The Glory of the Loire

The Glory of the Loire

text by **Eugène Pépin**
photographs by **Hélène Jeanbrau**
translated by **Thomas Wikeley**

A STUDIO BOOK
The Viking Press · New York

La Loire au fil de ses châteaux

Published in 1971 by The Viking Press, Inc.
625 Madison Avenue, New York, N.Y. 10022

SBN 670–34262–9
Library of Congress catalog card number: 79–150357

Color illustrations printed in France
Text and monochrome illustrations printed in Great Britain
by Jarrold and Sons Ltd, Norwich
Bound in Great Britain

Contents

Preface *by Maurice Genevoix, Permanent Secretary of the French Academy*

Balzac said that 'the best Florentine painter had never been near Florence'. If that is true, I am guilty of some temerity. For if I have written so much about the Loire it is because I was born on its banks, between its arms rather, on an island (at Decize, 'a little town on the Loire seated'). My life has been spent near it, on its banks, its rocks, barefoot in its swift currents or swimming in the deep *mouilles* where the summer eddies swirl; my childhood was entirely surrendered to and steeped in the place. I have no more need to go there than I have to go to the air I breathe and by which I live. I have only to lift my eyes to encompass in one look through the branches of the poplars, just bared by the winds of autumn, the wide, calm mirror of the river lapping at the foot of our house, the beaches darkening at the edges with waters which will soon cover them again; and the vale spread out beyond, ochre and pale at this season, studded with small farms, brown roofs, red roofs, and groups of trees pierced by slender belfries, and the horizon stretching away southward to the blue, almost transparent, long line of the birch- and pine-clad hills of Sologne melting into the half-light.

Today the light is grey, grey and blue; grey and blue the immense stretch of sky where the vague, white transparencies of the clouds extend like the banks of an aerial river and are reflected in the pearly surface of the waters; and it is all sweet softness, fine and subtle, sieved by the light of the invisible sun; I need but close my eyes to feel the full force of its friendly presence.

I would like to tell a tale from the past which is not out of place because, more than appears, it is of concern to the people of these menacing times. Barbarity terribly scarred those of my generation whom it did not ki outright. I remember scenes of horror in a setting itse distorted. No more hills, no more horizons. Fountai of earth, dark and fragmented things turning throug the air in the light of conflagrations, haversacks, pieces human bodies, bits of broken pit props; a monstrou shell hitting the rear parapet, hitting at the same time th back of my neck and my chest, making me feel tha were I to touch my body with my hands, my han would feel my heart and lungs laid wide open; shout shadows dragging themselves along and groaning; an against my body, in a momentary cessation of noise, th gurgling of blood welling out of and dripping under th human bodies pressing against me, which leant again me an instant earlier in fear and a mad desire to live, an the inert weight gets heavier and suddenly becomes intolerable; rain, mud sucking one down, night fallin the heartrending cries for help from the wounded in bomb crater as the mud slowly closes over them; th bombardment resuming, hitting us and making the mu shudder to its unclean depths, something cold an slightly sticky slipping through my fingers, a piece human flesh lying there surrounded by slivers of stee What loneliness! At nightfall a passing runner pants ou to me that Porchon had just been killed, Porchon, th comrade of my earliest years, my brother in danger, th source of courage and hope. Entering a forward dressing station to have a shrapnel wound on his forehead tende he was struck by another shell that killed him as he pu his foot on the threshold.

I saw again in a living world, under an instantly remembered fresh, pure sky barely misted by the breath

e unseen river, the towers of the Holy Cross at rléans, swifts in sweeping flight above the courtyard our school, and the stone quays sloping gently down , yes, to the Loire itself. There were the plane trees of e Chastaing, the avenue of my own home town, the ght suspension bridge slowly bending between its bles to the passage of a firewood cart, the rotunda of e Penthièvre family mansion with the mansard roofs its stables, and finally the waters, the rosy beaches here the river laps, the gently ruffled rushes and the ver-blue leaves of the willows suddenly shaken by the eeze out of the west.

It was the whisper of the breeze in the willows which livered me that night from the horror and the din. It s since then always spoken to me of beautiful things, ltivated fields with the changing pink of flowering over and lightened by the rising corn; of Germigny-s-Prés and its venerable little church, of Saint-Benoît-r-Loire and its basilica where, on that same night, I nsed the union of the human with the divine.

I have covered the whole length of the Loire from erbier-des-Joncs to Donges, and hardly one of my eps was not that of a pilgrim. It is that river, those certi-des, which I have found again in these pages. These aters bear witness to a human ideal again threatened by esh barbarism. Beyond the happiness, and also perhaps e pride which they arouse, one could wish that they ight teach us a lesson.

I believe that there is hardly a region in the world here human civilization has imprinted itself more eply than in this wide valley with its gentle changes of pect and soil between one section and the next; a poetry is distilled from its stone monuments and the old flint walls of the boating and fishing villages, and poetry arises from the Loire itself. It is because of this that I am anxious, that I tremble for the other, the poetry of civilization to which man has owed the purest beauty, the noblest works achieved within that harmony of the skies and of the moving waters, the passing seasons, the splash of a wicker trap thrown back into the water by a fisherman, blackbirds singing in my garden hedge, the dialect of a vine-dresser from Blois, or the silky sound of icicles tinkling in a winter's night.

It has taken only half a century, a fleeting moment in time, for the apocalyptic cloud to rise above our heads and threaten to break upon us. We are repeatedly told that technological progress is by its own nature 'irreversible', that we cannot circumscribe it and must, consequently, accept it. I have only to open my eyes to start trembling, like an animal sensing the coming storm, at the thought of humanity teetering on the brink of a new abyss of horror. We are preparing a tragedy for ourselves beside which the *Centuries* of Nostradamus are no more than puerilities.

Vlaminck once told me that a little before 1914 he went with Derain into Paul Guillaume's picture gallery to the preview of an exhibition of cubistic paintings, a style still in its infancy at that time. Having looked at the pictures and listened to the learned commentary of gentlemen whom he irreverently called the 'financiers of the mystery', he found himself outside on the pavement alone with his friend. Both were flabbergasted, but Vlaminck differently from Derain; the latter was intrigued, interested, Vlaminck indignant and fulminat-

Following page
osier beds on the banks of the Loi

ing, and suddenly he prophesied, 'We are going to have a war, a world war!'

He told me another story . . . of his acrobat room-mate in the army. Like the Juggler of Notre-Dame in the monastery chapel, the room-mate again and again went through his repertoire in the closed barrack-room, with only Vlaminck to watch. He walked on his hands, somersaulting impeccably backwards and forwards, starting all over again, quickening to a mad pace, and then suddenly stopping dead. 'What's wrong?' Vlaminck asked, and the other replied, 'Nothing's wrong yet, but it was time to stop: I could no longer feel myself turning.'

But what have all these stories to do with the Loire? I have not deserted it and a fishing-rod will bring me back to it. Only fifty years ago, what a wealth of fish there was! The wonderful variety of native species! Bleak, roach, bream, carp, long-snouted pike lurking under the weeds, green perch with black stripes and red fins tacking around the piers, groups of barbel wallowing on the sandy bottoms, gudgeon poking among the gravel, a long line of chub in the rushes or under overhanging branches, their turned-up noses waiting for a fallen beetle or a mayfly brought low by the wind; they were all fish of the Loire. Today, they exist no more.

Sick with so much pollution, they have turned belly u
and rotted. No more schools of bleak skitter along th
water or jump in the moonlight. The curlews, too, a
going, and the great herons with their dangling legs an
slow, powerful wingbeats, and the arrow-like king
fishers, the circling martins and the swallows cutting th
wavelets as they pass. It is true that attempts are bein
made to restock the Loire, and that records are kep
counts taken, fisheries planned and programmed.

Progress once took the time and had the leisure t
check its own audacities, but today the pace is quicker
ing, and the devotees of progress are showing the fir
symptoms of the staggers – a deadly malady of shee
What a catastrophe if the Loire also obeys the laws
progress, becoming the slave of future supermen,
reserve of *productive* (and lucrative) energy, a string
watery surfaces for outboard motors and water-skis!

To discipline and control life is fine, it is what huma
beings are for; but our first duty is to respect life. It is m
hope that the rising generations of the future civilizatio
fortunate products of test-tubes and the sole, gre
State-controlled school of minutely supervised high
education, will find in these pages more than a nosta
gia; they should find a stimulating invitation to fe
themselves 'turning' once more.

Introduction

The Loire is the longest river in France, with a course of about six hundred miles, draining an area extending over nearly one-quarter of the country. This vast region, however, has never had any real geographical unity; on the contrary, it consists of three clearly differentiated zones divided not only by their geological structure, the general aspect of the country, the climate and the human habitat, but also by the events of their history. The only factor shared by the three zones is the irregular flow of the river, too much water alternating with too little, which has prevented the Loire from becoming an important channel of communication, even though navigation has been possible at certain times over a long stretch of the river.

The upper reaches of the Loire, as far downstream as Bec d'Allier, are shut in by the ancient rocks at the edge of the Central Plateau, which have been overlaid by lava and ashes from volcanic eruptions. This is the *Loire of the Mountains*, running for the most part through deep, narrow gorges over which the ruins of feudal châteaux stand guard; volcanic or granitic sills divide the valley into a succession of basins, some of considerable dimensions, such as in the Forez and the Roannais. This part of the river has no very important centres of population, Saint-Etienne and Le Puy having developed some distance away. The climate of this reach is harsh during a great part of the year. With the exception of the big industrial complex of Saint-Etienne, it is essentially a farming region, with stock-breeding in the Velay highlands and agriculture on the lower slopes. The torrential flow of the Loire in th high valley has always been a bar to navigation, but th surrounding tablelands have for centuries been a mear of communication between the Mediterranean Sea an the Parisian river basin; indeed, evidence of souther influence and linguistic reminders of the *Langue d'* are to be found in this region.

Towards Decize and Digoin the countryside changes it becomes the transitional point between the rugge area upstream and the more peaceful region below th Bec d'Allier. Centres of population come closer to th river; some were active river ports until quite recently From the confluence with the Allier as far as Ponts-de Cé the river flows for about 250 miles in a wide, gentl sloping valley without serious interruptions; along thi reach, protected by 'levees', important centres of market gardening and other produce have sprung up, as well a rich orchards and excellent grazing lands; vineyards ar thick on the slopes above the right bank as well as th left, even overflowing down into the bottom of th valley, particularly south of Orléans. The maritim climate prevailing over this entire region greatly favour such agricultural development: winters are relativel mild and summers never too hot. Poets have sung c 'la douceur angevine' ('the Anjou sweetness') an 'Touraine, the garden of France'. The inhabitants are serious people, full of good sense enlivened with flashe of cheerfulness and wit; the *Langue d'oïl* prevai throughout the region in all its richness and purity.

Christianity came early to the valley, which is full c

churches, often reconstructed or enlarged; powerful abbeys here became focal points for the spread of civilization. On several occasions this middle stretch of the Loire could rightly claim to be called the Royal Loire; the Orléannais, often the residence of Carolingian kings in the tenth century, was the cradle of the Capetian dynasty; about the same time, dynasties of counts, later to produce kings of England, established themselves in Touraine and Anjou. There for nearly two hundred years from the beginning of the fifteenth century, the kings of France governed the country from their residences in Touraine or the Blésois. During that period, châteaux and sumptuous residences were built in the valley of the Loire and its vicinity, or were modernized n accordance with the taste of the time. This is the reach of the river rightfully known as the *Loire of the Abbeys ind Châteaux*.

For a long time before railways were built, the river carried a great deal of traffic, in spite of the varying level of its waters, thus providing easy communications beween the centre of France and the *Loire of the Sea*. In this hird sector of its course the Loire again comes into conact with ancient rock formations of schist and granite, hrough which it has to force its way to reach the sea. There has always been a certain amount of river traffic etween the river port of Angers and Nantes. All the ctivities of this region, however, are directed towards he sea; the estuary, which is a gateway for raw materials nd petroleum products, is the site of a vast and conantly expanding industrial zone.

The Loire of the Mountains

etween the Vivarais and the Velay, in the middle of the ivarais hills, the Mézenc massif rises to a height of arly six thousand feet. One of the summits is the erbier-des-Joncs, a perfect cone of chaotically piled-up ck completely bare of vegetation. The source of the oire is on the southwest side of the Gerbier. The huge ézenc massif, rising over a base of primitive rocks, as produced by eruptions of phonolitic matter in the iocene period, which separated the basin of the Loire om that of the Rhône and of which an outflow extends far as Mount Mégal, almost in the centre of the Velay. ere, the two bare horns of the Mézenc stand above ntle slopes, which attract devotees of snow sports ring the long winter months and which, in spring, are rpeted with thousands of flowers, principally gentians d violets. Sheep prefer the grass of these fields, mixed it is with aromatic plants, to that in the valleys below; d the rugged mountain cowherds bring to pasture re their herds of black or brown-and-white cattle. he Mézenc plateau is studded with rounded volcanic nes known as *sucs*.

The Loire rises from the foot of the Gerbier in a slop- g, bush-strewn meadow. Today, the waters of the oire Spring', canalized and imprisoned as soon as they pear, pour out of a narrow pipe into a stone trough der the porch of a low house said to be six centuries d. From there the little trickle of water slips round the ot of the walls and runs down into the fields. The tle house, with the pompous name of 'Ferme de la oire', is typical of the houses of the high Vivarais: ctangular buildings of undressed, black or reddish lava ocks, with high chimneys solidly built to withstand

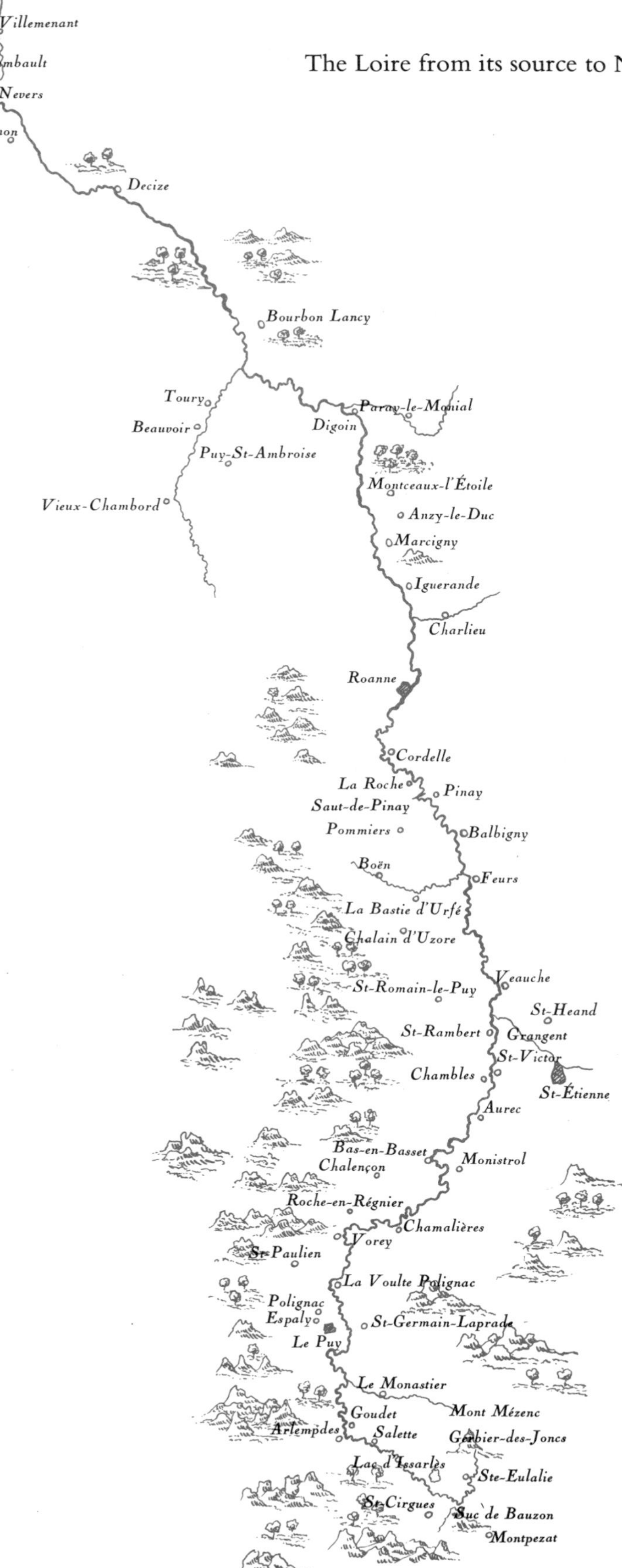

The Loire from its source to Neve

the winds; the fairly steeply sloping roofs are covered with the flat, grey-blue micaceous stones derived from the neighbouring phonolites. Backing on to a rise giving protection from the cold north wind, the house has openings only towards the south, where there are narrow windows and the only door; the latter is sheltered by a porch giving protection from accumulations of snow. Animals and people live together in the house.

The 'Ferme de la Loire', which is flanked by two modern buildings serving as restaurants, is the starting-point for the climb to the top of the Gerbier-des-Joncs, from whose summit one can see a wide panorama, except towards the north where the view is blocked by the broad mass of Mount Mézenc. To the south and west, beyond the high valley of the Loire, the volcanic peaks of the Massif Central are visible; on the eastern horizon the snowy chain of the Alps looms over the winding gorges of the Eysse, a tributary of the Erieux, and the steep slopes of the Vivarais run down towards the valley of the Rhône.

The rivulet of the Loire at first runs south, as if it were destined to continue towards the Rhône valley and on to the Mediterranean. Winding through the wide valley of Sainte-Eulalie it runs, in normal weather, in a narrow bed encumbered with rocks, but when the snow melts or after heavy rain, it overflows its banks and, like all the small rapids joining it, carries along with it pebbles, sand and bits of rock. Sainte-Eulalie is the site of an annual Violet Fair to which people come from afar to buy medicinal plants gathered in the mountains. After some eight miles the rivulet encounters the Suc de Bauzon with its beautiful pine-and-beech forest adjoining one of

House at the source of the river

e first tributary stream

The Loire from the bridge at La Borie

the most rugged regions of the Cevennes between tl Loire, the village of Burzet and the source of tl Fontolière, a tributary of the Ardèche. To the south, tl Suc de Bauzon dominates the little lake of Ferrand an beyond it, the Pal pass, said to be the route most used ancient times between the Rhône basin and that of tl Loire; there is a tradition that Julius Caesar crossed tl Cevennes at this place on his way to attack the reb Vercingetorix.

Prevented from continuing its way southward, tl Loire turns northeast through very deep gorges ar receives various tributaries carrying the heavy rai waters of the eastern slopes of the Cevennes; to the le is the Vernason, coming from the forest of Mazan ar flowing past the charming village of Saint-Cirgues-e Mazan where lace-makers still work beside the o Romanesque church; to the right the Gage and tl Veyradeyre, coming from the slopes of the Mézen flow through a region of a few hamlets and isolat farms. During the last twenty years this high valley the Loire has been profoundly changed by the creatic of the EDF's (Electricité de France) vast hydroelectr complex which makes use of the sharp difference level between the Loire and the Mediterranean slop Dams have produced reservoir-lakes. On the Loire, tl mighty dam of La Palisse stores up behind its gre height enormous quantities of water; on the Gage is tl narrow dam – it is said to be the narrowest in the world of Le Peyron; on the Veyradeyre, the reservoir of I Grange has formed behind another dam. The water th collected can be directed into Lake Issarlès, an in mense oval depression, one of the deepest in France, wi

rtified farm near Salette

ep slopes rising from it – in particular those of the lcano Cherchemus – the surface level of the water ing several hundred feet above that of the Loire bed. om Lake Issarlès an underground conduit about ten les long takes the water through to the Mediterranean pe as far as the Suc de Montasset, above the under-ound power house of Montpezat, which lies to the rth of the hamlet of Champagne. The Issarlès-ontpezat complex was completed in 1954 and had quired the labour of two thousand workmen over five ars. At the village of Issarlès, a summer resort on the e in which trout grow to a great size but do not breed, Loire has descended more than sixteen hundred feet er a distance of twenty miles from its source.

Between Issarlès and Le Puy are châteaux ruins along both banks of the river; for the most part they are perched on isolated pitons and, during the Wars of Religion, were taken and retaken by Calvinists, Ligueurs and Royalists. Today, these romantic ruins, often with small villages crouching at their feet, dominate the torrential course of the Loire with its steep, wooded banks and numerous bends along which no passable roads run. Particularly worthy of mention are: the picturesque fortified village of Arlempdes, its basalt gateway dating from 1066, the eleventh-century church with its trefoil doorway, and the ruins of an important fort with round and square towers, perched on a basalt rock; the village of Goudet with the ruins of Château

Ruins of the Château of Arlempdes
seen from the bottom of the gorge

Beaufort, guarding a ford in the bend of the Loire; t
village of Solignac, its twelfth-century church built
the edge of a basalt spur rising vertically above t
course of the river; the village of Cussac on the rig
bank, where the widening of the valley marks the begi
ning of the ancient Tertiary lake of Le Velay; the villa
of Goubon and its wall-belfry, and the fourteent
century keep of Château Poinsac in a bend of the Loir
the village of Bouzols and the ruins of a twelfth-centu
keep; the village of Brives-Charensac and the remains
its old sixteenth-century bridge near the junction wi
the Borne river at the gates of Le Puy.

Life may be difficult in these little villages in wint
but in summer their population is increased tenfold
visiting campers and summer residents who can aband
themselves to the joys of fishing not only in the Loi
but also in the numerous rapid streams running into
teeming with crayfish and mountain trout. Picturesq
roads with horseshoe bends lead from the bottom of t
narrow valley to the tableland above, with many po
sibilities for outings. On the left bank, a few miles furth
on, lies the almost circular lake of Le Bouchet, with t
clearest of water filling the bottom of a crater, su
rounded by wooded country. Not far away, the Cro
de la Chèvre and the Devès ridge provide some ea
climbs. On the right bank, three miles as the crow fl
from the gorges, the township of Monastier-su
Gazeille, its high houses roofed with rounded tiles gi
ing it a southern look, stretches along an escarpme
above grassy slopes running down to this small tributa
of the Loire. In the seventh century, Calminius, Cou
of Auvergne who was canonized under the name of

winding stretch of the Loire
en from the Château of Arlempdes

ıe ruined Château
Beaufort

he Organ of Espaly',
ar Le Puy

llowing pages:
ew of Le Puy-en-Velay

ılmin, chose for his retreat this spot not far from the ›man road leading from the Vivarais to Le Puy by ıy of Le Béage; around 680 he founded an important bey there. The existing abbey church is a beautiful ample of the Auvergnat style, not only because of the elfth-century Romanesque construction with its ·ade decorated with mosaics and polychrome – but ›stly red – stones, but also for its east end, which was :onstructed during the Gothic period; the treasury :ludes a twelfth-century reliquary-bust of silver, set th precious stones. The abbot's house, a solid, square ilding with corner towers, as well as part of the ;hteenth-century cloister, still stands behind the urch. On the plateau, with its vast pasturelands sur-ınding the little valley of the Gazeille, are the ordinary uses of the region, built of lava blocks, but occasion-y roofed with thatch instead of the blue-grey *lauzes* the region. The village of Estables, very close to the ırce of the river, is the highest commune of the ·partment of Haute-Loire.

ter all these rather austere tablelands and gorges, the ›in of Le Puy, watered by the river, seems an oasis. ıe town of Le Puy-en-Velay, at a short distance from : river, is built on an incomparable site, one of the ›st curious in France, at the bottom of a wide basin ·med by ancient volcanic activity and erosion, and ıbellished by the hand of man. The point on the rim the basin from which it can be seen as a whole, is on : road from Clermont through Brioude or from :hy by way of La Chaise-Dieu, above the 'Organ' of ›aly at the level of the Belvédère; it is a most extra-ordinary view. Out of the town with its black, red-roofed houses rise two remarkable rocks: the Aiguilhe Saint-Michel, a veritable obelisk of lava, and the Corneille hill, higher and more massive, on the side of which the cathedral has been built.

The top of the Aiguilhe is crowned by a chapel, the belfry continuing the vertical line into the sky in a way which Jules Romain, a son of the Velay, has called 'a challenge to good sense'. The chapel, now dedicated to St Michel, is thought to have replaced a temple first sacred to the Gaulish god Belenus and then to Mercury; during the Middle Ages, it was no less famous as a place of pilgrimage than the sanctuary of the Black Virgin, and pilgrims heading for St James of Compostella came to make their devotions here, climbing on their knees up the 240 steps cut into the rock, before setting out on their long journey. An oratory was first built here in 962. Above this early building, under which the rock itself breaks the surface, the existing monument was built at the end of the eleventh century; to it was added, at the end of the twelfth century, a charming polychrome façade comprising a door beneath a trefoil arch, showing southern and Moorish influence. Its interior is decorated with wall-paintings dating from different periods and, in 1955, the original altar was restored to its place.

The people of Le Puy consider the cathedral the real centre of the town; beneath it the upper town spreads out, with houses of the old nobility with decorated façades and inner courtyards on both sides of its narrow streets. Once surrounded by fortifications, of which the old Panessac Tower is the best-preserved remnant, the

Rood-screen, Le Puy cathedral

town was regarded as a holy place during the Middle Ages. During the Roman period it was known as 'Anicium' or Mount Anis. Tradition has it that there was a temple of Diana – which is perhaps corroborated by the existence of a bas-relief depicting a hunting scene – and this temple was perhaps built on the site of a druidic sanctuary, whose 'fever stone' – the reason for the pilgrimage to Le Puy – is still in the lower part of the narthex and is still venerated.

The old chronicles of the Velay relate that at the end of the third century the Virgin appeared to a poor widow of the neighbourhood suffering from a malig-

nant fever and told her to go to the hill of Anis and l down on a megalithic stone slab there. The wom obeyed, and rose cured. Two centuries later, a paralys man from the village of Ceyssac was also cured aft having lain upon the same stone; when the Virg appeared again, she is said to have asked for a church be built on the spot. St Vosy, Bishop of the Vela whose see was then at 'Ruessium' – now called Sain Paulien – capital of the Velay, went off to Rome request the transfer of his see to Mount Anis; he broug back from Rome a certain senator and architect who name, Scutarius, is cut into the stone of the 'For' porc

Lace-making

on the south side of the cathedral; he is believed to have built the original sanctuary in the last years of the fifth century.

In the seventh century the powers of the bishops began to increase. From the tenth century on it was the king of France who had the right to appoint the bishop, although the bishopric was still included in the domains of the counts of Auvergne, themselves vassals of the dukes of Aquitaine; in 923, the bishops first induced the counts of Auvergne and the Velay to relinquish all their rights over the town of Anis and then, in 927, persuaded King Raoul to grant to them the right of minting money. By 1025, the pilgrimage had already become famous, and it seems that it was about then that the name of Puy-Sainte-Marie replaced that of Anis.

About that date also the fame of St James of Compostella crossed the Pyrenees, and it was a bishop of Le Puy, by name of Gorescalc, who became the first French pilgrim of St James. Thereafter, the prosperity of Le Puy continued to increase, not only because of the pilgrimage to the cathedral itself, but also because it became an assembly-point for pilgrims making for St James, since it lay on the route through the Cevennes by way of Conques and Moissac which was taken by the pilgrims from Burgundy and the east of France towards the passes of the Pyrenees.

Little remains of the early sanctuary; a new building was begun in the eleventh century to meet the growing needs of the pilgrimages, the fame of which became even greater in the twelfth century, thanks to the arrival of the Black Virgin, a statue in cedar-wood no doubt brought by a crusader (it was burnt by the revolutionaries in 1794); in 1239 St Louis added a Holy Thorn to the cathedral's treasure.

In 794 Charlemagne came on pilgrimage, and throughout the whole of the Middle Ages popes, kings of France, lords, commanders-in-chief and knights ceaselessly journeyed to Le Puy. While Joan of Arc was with Charles VII at Chinon, her mother Isabelle Romée also visited the place with her two sons. During the twelfth and thirteenth centuries building went on constantly; the main edifice was enlarged and completed by a number of annexes, the cloisters, the mortuary chapel and the building known as the 'machicolated' building, to which were added charitable institutions (the Almshouse and the Penitents' Chapel). Because of the steepness of the slope, however, space was limited, and this motivated the extraordinary decision which the builders of the cathedral were forced to make. The western bays of the nave were built out into space and supported by pillars, while a monumental stairway, continuing the long ascent from the 'Tables', led below these bays through the Golden Door and ended at the High Altar. This arrangement was altered when the work of restoration and consolidation of 1781 was carried out; the stairway now stops at the Golden Door and two lateral staircases lead on one hand to the nave and on the other to the cloisters. Repairs were made during the nineteenth century, but the existing building as a whole is a fairly faithful replica of the cathedral as it was before the Revolution.

Apart from the polychrome façade which we owe to the restorers' skill, the series of octagonal cupolas on squinches above the nave is almost unique in this part of

Top left: detail of sculpture on the Saint-Michel d'Aiguilhe chapel at Le Puy

Details of sculpture on the 'For' Porch, Le Puy cathedral

France; the square belfry behind the apse, also, with its seven storeys is of the kind found in the Limousin. Two doorways complete the exterior. The one on the south side, known as the 'For' porch, contained the papal door reserved for visiting Roman pontiffs and is covered with interesting sculptures: among them, above some of the capitals, are what are thought to be representations of the seven deadly sins. The figure of a mermaid with two tails could stand for Lust; two eagles facing each other for Pride; a purse with its strings knotted for Avarice; a dog showing its teeth for Envy. A small figure high up on the west face, with bowed head and hands on knees, might represent Sloth. Kings princes and governors of Languedoc used to enter the cathedral by the north doorway, called the Saint-Jean porch, whose sculptures were altered in 1749.

The cathedral is a real museum of religious art, with frescoes in the transept galleries and in the canons library which represent the liberal arts, and those in the mortuary chapel which include a crucifixion and illustrations of Charlemagne's campaign in Spain according to the *Chanson de Roland*. Also noteworth are the 'cedar' doors dating from the middle of th twelfth century, with their delicate carvings, and th extraordinary wrought-iron screen, of the same period A precious example of Carolingian calligraphy, th Theodolph Bible, is kept in the treasury.

Compared to all these splendours the colossal statu of Notre-Dame-de-France, erected on top of th Corneille rock, in 1860 by public subscription, is onl of mediocre interest. From the lofty vantage-point c the top of the rock, or, better still, from the Virgin

Preceding pages:
the village of Espinasse

crown, a magnificent panorama can be enjoyed, not only of the basin of Le Puy, but of the whole Velay.

This high, vast basalt plateau, extending over a bed of crystalline rocks, is bristling with volcanic *sucs*; to the east, it abuts on the wooded chain of the Velay mountains, to the north it is bounded by the bend of the Loire along which run the southern foothills of the Forez mountains; to the east and south it stretches to the picturesque valley of Velay Lignon at the foot of the Boutières mountain chain, an extension of the Mézenc massif. Although sometimes considered part of the Auvergne, the Velay, with its circle of mountains, is in fact a distinct entity. During the Roman occupation the country of the Velay, with its old Gaulish capital Ruessium, was part of the Narbonnaise. Despite the transfer of the episcopal see to Mount Anis after it was sacked by the Barbarians in the sixth century, the city of Saint-Paulien retained a certain measure of importance throughout the Middle Ages thanks to pilgrimage to the much-venerated tomb of the bishop. Later, the early feudal period saw the rise all over the Velay of small local lordships with châteaux and fortified villages and the attempts of certain of the nobility to reduce the powers of the bishops of Le Puy, which continued until 1307, when a contract of association was concluded between the bishop and King Philip the Handsome, incorporating Le Velay in the domains of the Crown. Later, the Wars of Religion and, thereafter, the troubles with the League, brought about dissension among the people of the district who, for many months, refused to recognize Henry IV. Finally, on Richelieu's orders, several of the châteaux were dismantled.

Today the whole plateau, through which the Loi[re] and its tributaries have dug their beds, is entirely agr[i]cultural. There is one very special industry, howeve[r,] which since the sixteenth century has contributed [at] least as much as the pilgrimages to spreading the fam[e] of Le Puy and the Velay throughout the world – th[e] production of hand-made lace, mostly from line[n] thread. Particularly from the sixteenth century onwar[ds] women of the Velay chose this craft, which they coul[d] perform in their own homes. During certain perio[ds] there were as many as sixty or eighty thousand lace-makers in the Velay, but today competition fro[m] machine-made lace is too strong and apprentices are n[o] longer enrolled. In rural regions one can still see lace-makers at work on their low stools, with the 'pillow' o[n] their knees and bobbins dangling, but in the town of L[e] Puy, where before the last war crowds of them coul[d] be seen, especially on the 'Tables' in front of th[e] cathedral, they are becoming ever rarer.

After leaving the Le Puy basin the valley of the Loi[re] becomes a succession of narrows and small basin[s.] Pressed upon from one side by the lava flows from th[e] Velay mountains and from the other by those of th[e] Mézenc, the valley is broken up by rocky outcrops [of] great size. The river, which originally spread out [to] form temporary lakes, has had to open a new chann[el] for its waters through these basalt dikes. It is thus th[at] the magnificent 'gates', cut through the rock betwe[en] Peyredeyre and Lavoûte, have become the outlet for th[e] waters which filled the Le Puy basin in prehistor[ic]

The ancient castle fort of Polignac dominating the surrounding village

nes. These gorges also provide a passage for the road d the railway, whose construction required con- lerable feats of engineering. A nearly circular loop or *ulte* of the river surrounds the sheer rock on which s the Château of La Voulte-Polignac, the country sidence of the Polignac family since the thirteenth ntury. The valley then widens to form the small basin Emblavès between the villages of Beaulieu and Saint- ncent, and narrows again to flow round the spur nich bears the ruins of the Château of Caneuil. After ning with the Arzon near Vorey, the Loire turns arply eastwards to enter the defile of Chamalières. nere, the phonolitic strata of Mount Gerbison and of ount Miaune, which correspond exactly and in rlier times formed a single sheet, are today separated om each other by a great gash, which the Loire has wly cut through the layers of lava and granite.

Chamalières, with its mild climate and its situation se to pine woods, made its first appearance in history in the tenth century; the priory, formerly fortified, belonged to the Abbey of Monastier until the Revolution. The remarkable twelfth-century church, to which alterations were made in the eighteenth century, is in the style of the Auvergne; it was once flanked by a cloister built as a terrace along the bank of the river, but only the chapter-house survives. Inside the church are two objects of interest: an old monolithic pillar from the cloister composed of four column-statues of prophets, and the Romanesque cedar-wood church door, formerly encrusted with ivory, on which the figures of mounted warriors and fantastic animals can still be seen. Finally, following a Roman precedent, there are phonolite jars inserted in the masonry of the wide half-dome of the apse, put there, as in a number of other churches of the region, to improve the acoustics.

After flowing round the steep cliff crowned by the ruins of the Château of Artias, the Loire runs by the township of Retournac with its eleventh-century

Well-head at the Château
of Chalain d'Uzore

The Château of La Voulte-Polignac
overlooking the Loire

Countryside outside Le Puy

church of pleasantly coloured yellow sandstone. Th Loire then turns north-northwest, with the cliffs of th Forez mountains on its left bank and a beautiful cli road round the foot of Mount Madeleine, ending in th ancient, fortified township of Beauzac. The old wal of the latter are crowned with curious wooden gallerie and the church, with a wall-belfry, possesses one of th few crypts of the region with groined vaults supporte by small, slender columns with carved capitals (twelft century). After another bend, the Loire enters the sma Tertiary basin of the Basset, a wide plain between B and Monistrol, receiving on the left the waters of th Ance flowing down from the Forez mountains. Bo the Loire and the Ance are particularly rich in differe kinds of fish, such as perch, pike, carp and trout, makin Bas-en-Basset a paradise for fishermen. The majest ruins of the Château of Rochebaron, built during th reign of Charles VII, dominate the little town. In 121 the domain of Bas was given by Philippe Auguste to th Bishop of Le Puy, together with the Châteaux Chalençon and Chapteuil, but the Château of Roch baron soon returned to secular ownership and i masters took an active part in the wars of the Midd Ages. Facing Bas on the right bank of the rive Monistrol was one of the principal towns of the Vel and the property of the bishops of Le Puy, who made their summer residence. The present château, built 1475 by Bishop Jean de Bourbon and largely rebuilt the seventeenth century, has a façade flanked by tw enormous towers and is reached by a flight of ste which twice turns upon itself. The old gardens wi their avenues of lime trees form a terrace permitting

Ruins of the Château of Rochebaron
above Bas-en-Basset

e Château and village
Chalençon

e Devil's Bridge,
ar Chalençon

de view over the plain of Bas. The Church of onistrol, partially rebuilt in the seventeenth century, l has its Romanesque nave, with a dome over the nsept crossing. The town suffered during the troubled e of the League and from the exploits of the famous ron des Adrets.

After a broad bend, the Loire enters a series of gorges, th a cliff road on the left bank leading to Aurec, where arge stretch of water opens out towards the Forez.

The region stretching away from the left bank of the ire downstream from Le Puy is no less interesting n the valley itself. In the direction towards the Velay ountains, just beyond the west gate of Le Puy, a wide salt hillock bears the powerful fortress of Polignac. In man times there was a temple of Apollo here, famous its oracles, which was visited in AD 47 by the nperor Claudius. It is said that questions asked by grims at the foot of the hill could be heard through a ll by the priests of the temple above, who thus had ne to prepare their replies. In the tenth century, the ds of Polignac made the place their fortified strong-ld; in the thirteenth century an enclosing wall, or ceinte, which is still extant, was built around the per platform, in the centre of which is a rectangular ep built between 1385 and 1421 beside the seignorial idence. This impregnable position made the viscounts Polignac in the Middle Ages masters of the surround- country, although not without frequent trials of ength with the burgesses of Le Puy as well as with the hops of the Velay. Below the château, the often-odified Romanesque church possesses some precious rteenth-century frescoes.

A little further north we come to Saint-Paulien with its twelfth-century church; after considerable alterations and transformation into a fortified church with galleries, machicolations and a parapet walk, it remains a magnificent building if only for the width of its barrel-vault. Saint-Paulien still has numerous relics of the times when it was the old capital of the Velay, such as the 'bull-slaughter stone', which was probably a Gallo-Roman sacrificial altar. Beyond Saint-Paulien is the Château of Rochelambert, on a verdant site, which was immortalized by George Sand in the novel *John of the Rock*; backing on to the vertical wall of the Velay mountains, this Gothic building, dating from the fifteenth and sixteenth centuries, was partially burnt down during the Wars of Religion but has been well restored.

Still further north, on the slopes of Mount Borie, facing the lofty volcanic cone of Mount Bar, with its covering of beech trees, the houses and narrow little streets of Allègre rise in stages to the ruins of an important fourteenth-century fortress. Throughout this hinterland, well watered by rivers such as the Arzon, the Ance and their tributaries, there are beautiful meadows adjoining rye and wheat fields, as well as vineyards on the hill slopes. Ruins of many châteaux and fortified villages, such as the Château of Arzon on the river of the same name, can be seen and the very ancient village of Roche-en-Régnier, not far from the gorges of Chamalières, with its high tower dominating the surrounding plateau, which may be reached by a long, winding road. Then there are the Château and village of Chalençon on the higher reaches of the Ance, flowing in its wooded

Farmland near Aurec

ravine crossed by a narrow, medieval bridge known as the 'Devil's Bridge', once the boundary between the Velay and the Forez. Ten years ago, the houses of this walled township were falling to pieces and the inhabitants were leaving it, but eight years ago groups of young people started to work each summer under the direction of two priests, and with help from the public housing authorities have been trying to bring this village back to life without spoiling its picturesque aspect. The thirteenth-century château with its chapel, keep and walls is well preserved; formerly the property of the illustrious family of Chalençon, related to the Polignacs, it now belongs to the Polignac family and in 1969 provided the setting for several very successful performances of the pageant *Dramatic Nights of the Velay*.

The tablelands on the right bank of the Loire al watered as they are by numerous tributaries of which t longest is the Velay Lignon, are not without picturesq interest. The landscape presents a great variety aspects deriving from the juxtaposition of the effects volcanic activity during different epochs. As one com down from the tableland into the valley, the austerity pastoral hamlets gives way progressively to pleasa townships, from Saint-Julien-Chapteuil near Le Puy Montfaucon and Saint-Didier, which add 'en-Velay' their names. Numerous villages mark the course of t Lignon in its picturesque valley, where wooded gorg alternate with green meadows and vast stretches water such as that formed by the Lavallette dam; example, the village of Le Chambon, an active cen

View from Chambles of the Loire flowing through a series of gorges

˘ Protestantism, and Tence, with its solid granite ɔuses at the end of the higher gorges. In the lower ɔrges, Electricité de France have erected two dams pplying two power stations. The Lignon, previously ossed by a road from Le Puy to Saint-Etienne over an d bridge at the hamlet of Pont-de-Lignon, joins the ɔire almost opposite the remains of the priory of onfolens, perched on a vertical rock.

At Aurec begins the magnificent lake formed by the rangent dam, which has submerged the lower parts ˘ the gorges. This huge reservoir is fringed by villages ıd châteaux situated on rocky spurs jutting out over e gorges. On the right bank, the village of Saint-Paul- ı-Cornillon, crouching below a fourteenth- to teenth-century château, which is still inhabited, was the seat of one of the most important baronies of the Forez. Further along, Saint-Victor, with its Romanesque church and its sixteenth-century château on the edge of the twisting defile of the Lizeron, provides a magnificent view over the bend of the river running round the Châtelet peninsula.

On the opposite bank, there are similar broad views over the river bends from the terrace around the Church of Chambles, built on the site of an old château at the highest point of the gorges above the valley; the thirteenth-century wall and a very slim, round tower are still standing. Lower down, immediately upstream from the dam, are the ruins of the thirteenth-century Château of Issolois with its two bulky towers. The gorges, now filled by the Grangent reservoir, have

Lake reservoir at Grangent

always made it easy to defend the passage over the river between the Velay and the Forez. As far back as Gaulish times, a fortified town probably existed on a site called the 'Palace' atop the height above the Château of Issolois. From the twelfth century on, this passage was defended by the Château of Grangent, the ruins of which, with a high round tower and a chapel roofed with red tiles, today stand on an island which was a promontory before the waters cut through it. The dam, completed in 1957, serves to regulate the flow of the river, the waters of which are subject to sudden and often unforeseeable spates. Finally, the banks of the immense reservoir provide new places for relaxation and water sports.

The town of Saint-Etienne, only a few miles from the river, is the centre of a vast industrial area, with a population of 400,000; its coalmines, now becoming exhausted, and its metallurgic industries, including the production of sporting guns and bicycles, as well as its textile and ribbon industries, have all contributed to establish its renown. The town is also at the junction of two important roads: the 'Route Bleue' which joins Holland, Belgium and Paris to the Côte d'Azur, and the 'Route d'Argent' between Switzerland and the Basque country.

To the north of Saint-Etienne, the town of Saint-Héand lies in the foothills of the Lyonnais uplands bordering the plain of Forez; this town is universally known today because the photographic lenses which enabled the American cosmonauts to take magnificent pictures of the moon were made there.

★ ★ ★

Staircase and galle
Château of La Bastie d'U

The plain of Forez occupies the bed of a large ancient Tertiary lake between the Forez mountains to the west and the uplands of the Lyonnais to the east, and it has always been a geographical entity distinct from the big historical regions surrounding it: Bourbonnais, Bourgogne, Dauphiné, Languedoc, Provence, Auvergne. For this reason, ever since the Roman occupation, of which numerous traces survive – notably the many milestones – the Forez was attached successively to one or other of the neighbouring regions until the hereditary counts made their appearance in the tenth century. In 1441 they transferred their capital from Fleurs on the Loire to Montbrison; they had recognized the king of France as their sovereign as far back as 1173, but the Forez was not united to the Crown until 1531.

A large part of Forez plain, especially west of the Loire, is strewn with numbers of pools in process of drying out, with lush growths of reeds providing refuge for waterfowl and excellent shooting for sportsmen. An astonishing variety of agricultural products results from the great diversity of soils, from cereals grown on the rich alluvia of the river meadows to the pastures of the Forez mountains, culminating in Pierre-sur-Haute, where cheese (*fourme*) is made in the *jasseries*; one can easily understand Honoré d'Urfé's enthusiasm in the lyrical description in his *Astrée* (published between 1609 and 1617) of his beloved land of Forez: 'There is a country called Forez which, though small, contains what is rarest in Gaul; half plains and half mountains, both of which are so fertile and have such a temperate climate that the soil can produce whatever the labourer may desire.'

The Forez is also rich in thermal waters (Montror les-Bains, Saint-Romain-le-Puy and, in particul Saint-Galmier); exploitation of these waters has creat important glass-works. From this plain, with its gen slope to the north – which follows that of the und lying horizontal Tertiary deposits – small cones volcanic origin jut out here and there, such as Sai Romain-le-Puy, Marcilly, Montbrison, Uzore, Mo verdun, crowned with churches or châteaux arou which, in many instances, villages have developed. T church on top of the peak of Saint-Romain-le-Puy is particular archaeological interest: because of the gradi and lack of available space, the eleventh-centu builder – whose name is known to us: Aldebert – h first to build the overhanging crypt and then the ap numerous archaic carvings of animals and small scer have been inserted into the outer walls. The lar château adjoining the church was demolished in 16 on Richelieu's order. A little to the north of Montbriso the late-eleventh-century Church of Champdieu, w its high defensive galleries and a parapet walk is ratl unusual; they were built in the fourteenth century.

In its course through the Forez, the Loire is joined a number of tributaries, though none of much impo tance. The Lignon, however, deserves special menti because of its influence on the literature of the 'Bergeri in the seventeenth century. Coming from Pierre-su Haute through the Forez mountains, where it pas close to the ruins of Couzan, this river reaches the pl at the ancient fortified town of Boen and waters t meadows of La Bastie d'Urfé before flowing into t Loire above Balbigny. La Bastie was a feudal manor

Saint-Romain-le-Puy
surmounting a volcanic plug

The ancient priory of Pommiers

'he Loire between the Pinay falls and La Roche

ıe fourteenth century but was remodelled in the ıfteenth century by Pierre d'Urfé, bailiff of the Forez nd chancellor to the Duke of Bourbon. In the sixteenth entury, important alterations were made by Claude 'Urfé who, as French ambassador in Rome during the alian Wars, had been won over by the Italian Renaisınce. Avoiding major changes to the buildings in the outhwest part of the courtyard, Claude extended them y a long gallery which he then enlarged on the courtard side into a monumental Italian-style loggia; the ›wer storey is a series of arches supported on fluted ılasters, and the wooden roof of the upper storey rests ı a classical cornice carried on small, elegant stone olumns, also fluted and topped by vaguely Corinthian ıpitals. The upper floor is reached by a gentle ramp ırrying a balustrade of small pillars in front of the ıllery and ending in a sort of pavilion which forms a orch. This group of buildings, exceptional in French enaissance architecture, is perhaps the work of a local master-mason after plans by Claude d'Urfé. The château contains two other novelties: the grotto and the chapel. The rock-work grotto, whose effect is enhanced by fountains, is an Italian fantasy analogous to the grotto in the Pine Garden at Fontainebleau; its date of 1550 makes it one of the earliest built in France, and it is one of the best preserved. Walls, ceiling and floor are composed of decorative, coloured gravel, shells and various kinds of stones. Beside it stood the completely Italianate chapel, once extremely sumptuous, with carved woods and marquetry panelling; unfortunately, a great deal of this decorative material was removed in the nineteenth century; at present the History Society of Montbrison is making efforts to restore the chapel. Honoré d'Urfé, grandson of Claude and author of *Astrée*, occasionally resided at La Bastie.

Another tributary of the Loire, the Aix, rising in the Bois-Noirs, a prolongation of the Forez mountains, flows by Saint-Germain-Laval and close to the priory of

A placid stretch of the Loire near La Roche

Ox-drawn plough in a field near Cordelle

›ommiers. The latter was founded in the eighth century ınd until the Revolution remained under the authority ›f Cluny through the intermediary of the monks of Nantua Abbey. The wall with its round towers and ortified gates encloses a somewhat austere-looking hurch, founded at the beginning of the eleventh entury by a count of the Forez as an act of reparation – s legend has it – for the murder of his daughter, Ste rève, whose body had supposedly been thrown into a vell. Acoustical pottery jars were built into the barrel-ault as in the church at Chamalières.

Emerging from the so-called Gorges of Saint-Victor, ıe Loire slows down and crosses the Forez for some wenty-five miles from south to north, 'not swollen and roud, but peaceful and calm' (*Astrée*). It flows past 'eauche and its eleventh-century church, Montrond-s-Bains, dominated by the ruins of a fourteenth-entury château, Feurs, which for some years was the apital of the newly established Department of the oire, and, finally, Balbigny. In the eighteenth century rtain work was done to make this part of the river avigable and *sapines*, heavy flat-bottomed boats built Saint-Rambert, were used to transport coal as well as ine from the Saint-Etienne region to Roanne and en to Nantes; the pilots who took the boats through e dangerous defiles of Pinay and Le Perron used to nbark at Balbigny.

The river encounters another obstacle formed by the cient rocks of the Neulize massif, through which it s to flow for twenty-five miles in winding gorges, ›t so deep as those upstream but just as beautiful. The ost striking part of the narrows occurs at the Pinay falls, the level of which was raised in 1711 when, by order of Louis XIV, a dike was built to control the floods which had previously wreaked havoc in the Orléannais and in Touraine. At the modern Château of La Roche the river becomes calm again and even widens at the foot of the château ruins of Saint-Maurice. On the banks, yoked white oxen work the rich alluvial soil, and the transition from the Forez to the Roannais becomes evident. But the Loire still has to overcome the rapids of the Perron falls, and it is only at Villerest that it finally leaves the gorges.

The town of Roanne is a few miles from Villerest, and in the Gallo-Roman period it was already an important crossroads and mentioned in the *Tabula Peutingeriana*. In the Middle Ages, when it was fortified and protected by an eleventh-century fortress of which the keep survives, the town was the property successively of the counts of the Forez, Jacques Cœur, the dukes of Bourbon and the counts of the Roannais. Having suffered a great deal during the Wars of Religion, throughout which it remained a Catholic town, Roanne experienced an intellectual revival in the seventeenth century; it also became a commercial town, thanks to its position both as a crossroads half-way between Lyons and the Loire, by way of Tarare, and as a river port for water-buses or *cabanes* carrying passengers and goods; in 1638, the town gained access to Paris when the Briare canal was opened. In the nineteenth century Roanne became an industrial town and from 1838, when the Roanne–Digoin canal was opened, its activity as a port increased.

Misericord on a stall in the church at Ambierle

Carving on a stall
in the church at Ambierle

For some years now, however, the tonnage of goods carried by water has tended to decrease as the result of competition from railways and road transport; the only remaining water traffic goes via the Roanne–Digoin canal, as there has been no traffic on the Loire since 1959, although the river is still listed as 'navigable', as far as La Noirie in the middle of the gorges.

The plain of Roanne, wider, richer and more prosperous than the Forez, stretches out from the left bank and even runs to the northwest up to the bend of the river, where it hits the Morvan heights after passing Digoin. Here the meadows provide excellent pastures, where herds of white cattle find grazing as rich as that of the Charollais region. The plain abuts to the west upon the porphyritic massif of the Madeleine mountains, which separate it from the valley of the Besbre, another tributary of the Loire. These mountains emerge from the Forez mountain chain at the peak of Montonce north of the col of Saint-Priest-le-Prugne and Sain Just-en-Chevalet; the recent discovery of uraniu deposits will bring new wealth to this region. The Bo de l'Assise is the highest point of the Madeleine chai which is paralleled to the west of Roanne by a line high ground called the 'Côte', which continues towar the north and then slopes more gently towards th Bourbonnais. The Côte and the eastern flanks of th Madeleine mountains, whence small tributaries of th Loire – such as the Renaison and the Teissonne – rus down through deep, shady ravines, are covered wi vines well exposed to the sun, growing around charn ing villages; the inhabitants are hospitable, as in all win producing regions.

From south to north along the Madeleine mountai a succession of buildings and towns bears witness to th

tistic past of this region. First, there is Saint-André-Apchon and its sixteenth-century church in the amboyant style, with lovely glass windows. A few iles to the north, the fortified town of Renaison under e joint lordship of the Count of the Forez and the ior of Ambierle, produced wines much appreciated ıring the seventeenth and eighteenth centuries in Paris here they were known as the wines of Arnaison. The hâteau of Boisy rises almost at the foot of Renaison; severe exterior – with a square fourteenth-century ep, a massive round tower with a pointed roof and achicolated curtain-walls – contrasts with its cheerful terior. This dwelling, which had belonged to Jacques œur, Superintendent of Finances under Charles VII, as reconstructed in the sixteenth century by Arthur ouffier, companion of Louis XII in Italy and, later, François I, thanks to whose favour he became Duke of the Roannais. The beautiful, arcaded gallery of the interior courtyard is perhaps a memento of Italy.

North of Renaison, after Saint-Haon-le-Châtel, purchased by Jacques Cœur, and after Saint-Haon-le-Vieux, is the Priory of Ambierle, well worth a stop. Clothilde, Clovis' widow, is thought to have founded an abbey on this spot, which in 938 became a priory of Cluny and was destroyed by fire at the end of the Hundred Years' War. Reconstruction of the priory buildings took place in the eighteenth century, and they now house schools and the town hall. They are dominated by the magnificent church, which we owe to the liberality of a prior *in commendam*, namely Antoine Balzac d'Entragues, who insisted on remaining prior despite his elevation to the episcopate and who devoted all his income to the construction of the church. It was built all in one spurt of activity during the last quarter of the fifteenth century in the Flamboyant style, but it betrays clear Burgundian influence; it is remarkable for the height of the nave. The high, triple windows contain splendid stained glass of extraordinary technical perfection, all made in the same workshop and portraying tall figures of bishops around a realistic Crucifixion. On the fifteenth-century altar is a carved and gilded wooden retable, given to the church by an official of the court of Burgundy and now again in its original place; the paintings on the six volets are attributed to Roger van der Weyden. Finally, among the fifteenth-century carved panels of the choir stalls there are curious carvings on the reveals of Adam, and of Eve with a child in her arms, both dressed in animal skins.

On the banks of the Teissonne we find the Cistercian Abbey of Benissons-Dieu, founded in 1138 by St Bernard; its church has a Romanesque nave with an ogival vault, which an abbot *in commendam*, Pierre de la Fin, covered with varnished tiles in 1460, at the same time as he built a high, free-standing tower.

Several miles north of Ambierle, the village of Crozet, with its medieval encircling walls, possesses a large, round, twelfth-century keep and many old wood and stone houses, including that of the lawyer Papon, which is covered with Latin apothegms.

To the east of the Roanne plain, the course of the Loire is bordered by hills much lower than the average altitude of the Madeleine mountains, their highest point being Crozan; the river here is of considerable width but of very varying depth and its bed is obstructed by sills and sandbanks. The flow of water may vary greatly, and when it is in flood the river is not navigable; the

Roanne–Digoin canal, however, runs parallel with th river's left bank and is joined by a lateral canal furth along. On the heights overlooking the Loire numero churches were built mostly as the result of prodding b the abbots of Cluny, whose abbey church, of which no hardly anything remains, was the largest in Christendo prior to the building of St Peter's in Rome. Some these churches are veritable art museums.

About ten miles north of Roanne and a short distan away from the Loire, on the lower course of its tributar the Sornin, lies the township of Charlieu; in the Midd Ages it was an important centre on the 'Great Loi Road' joining Lyons to Nevers on the way to Paris; i stone bridge is mentioned in the town's charters. Th township developed around a monastery founded 872 by Ratbert, a bishop of Valence who was the feud overlord of the locality; in 932 it became a priory Cluny and it was probably the great Abbot Odilon c Mercœur who reconstructed it in the first half of th eleventh century, although the reconstruction was n finished at his death. During the Revolution, everythin was razed to the ground, with the exception of the tw storey narthex, dating from the twelfth century, and th lower part of the first bay of the nave. Excavations 1926 brought to light the foundations of a succession earlier churches. The sculptures in the narthex, whic have fortunately survived, justify the title sometim given to the Church of Saint-Fortunat: 'The mo lavishly adorned daughter of Cluny.' Some see in th three arches of the north doorway the 'swan song' Cluniac sculpture; on the lintel, where Christ is show between two angels and surrounded by the apostles,

Adam and Eve, carvings on the reveals in the church at Ambierle

the famous representation of Lust in the form of a woman with a snake coiled around her and a toad devouring her breast; in the tympanum above, Christ is shown in an almond-shaped nimbus, supported by two angels and surrounded by the symbols of the Evangelists. The small doorway on the right, unfortunately much mutilated, shows a group of carvings of extraordinary workmanship; the lintel carries a scene of sacrifice in the antique manner, above a magnificently realistic representation of the Wedding at Cana; in the vault, a Transfiguration depicts Christ among St James, St Peter, St John, Moses and Elijah. Of the priory buildings, standing in an enclosure with a wall separate from that of the town, all that remains is the prior's house, a round tower and some lesser towers. The late thirteenth-century Church of St Philibert in the town is the only example of early Gothic in the Roannais.

From Pouilly-sous-Charlieu, close to the mouth of the Sornin, downstream as far as the Diou defile above the mouth of the Besbre, the Loire describes a broad curve, with Digoin at its centre. The river bed here would be wide enough to deal with heavy floods if it were not obstructed by sills and sandbanks. Along the left bank extends the plain of Roanne, with the Roanne–Digoin canal running parallel to the river; a succession of villages, churches and châteaux stand on the hills bordering the right bank, beside the railway and roads which follow the line of the valley. First along this roac is the Brionnais region, stretching from Charlieu in tl south to Paray-le-Monial in the north and abutting c the Beaujolais highlands to the east. The granitic subsc is covered with large meadows which have thick hedg around them and groups of trees to provide midd shelter for the animals. This is pastoral country *p excellence*, where numerous herds of white-and-t cattle are put to graze; important cattle marts are he in the region, such as the fat-stock market at Sair Christophe-en-Brionnais where the hurdy-gurdy us to be played.

In the eleventh and twelfth centuries, the influence the rich and powerful rule of the Brionnais extend over the whole of this region, reaching even beyond t Loire towards Iguerande and Marcigny. The capital the district, the old city of Semur-en-Brionnais, w first destroyed by the Barbarians in the fifth century a later suffered greatly, like all the region around during the Hundred Years' War and the Wars Religion. Abbot St Hugh, the great builder of Clu and Paray-le-Monial, was a member of the Sem family, and it is therefore not surprising that the coun is covered with Romanesque churches of Clun inspiration with plentiful sculptures and carvings. T influence of the Brionnais workshops extended very afield; it can be traced to beyond Charolles in the chu at Perrecy-les-Forges, where the doorway of

Porch details,
church at Charlieu

Left and opposite:
details of capitals
in the church at Anzy-le-Duc

Bosses on the Mill Tower at Marcigny

arthex is one of the most remarkable in Burgundy; egun in 1108, it foreshadows Vézelay.

On the right bank, the Loire passes first by Iguerande, ith its massive church perched on a sharply rising hill, ıd then Marcigny, an ancient fortified township ossessing a château built in the sixteenth century by the ıkes of Burgundy and partially destroyed in 1603. bbot St Hugh founded a priory there in 1065, of which ıe imposing fifteenth-century Mill Tower, now a ıuseum, survives; the walls are decorated with ırious bosses.

A short distance from the river stands the magnificent bbey Church of Anzy-le-Duc in the valley of the rconce, a tributary of the Loire with its source in the ools of the Charollais plateau; it flows past Charolles ıd for its last twelve miles runs parallel to the Loire. ıe Anzy priory, a dependency of Saint-Martin of ıtun, was founded by Hugh of Poitiers, a monk of int-Martin and a friend of Bernon, the first Abbot of uny. Hugh died in 930 and the veneration bestowed his relics by growing numbers of the faithful otivated the erection of a lovely church in the venth century; the choir and transept were probably ilt between 1000 and 1050 and the nave between 50 and the beginning of the twelfth century. Happily, church came through the Revolution undamaged, ile the priory buildings, often sacked or burnt in the urse of the ages, became private houses. This church s a nave of five bays flanked by side aisles, a projecting nsept and an apsidal choir; the latter extends into a all, centrally placed additional apse, with similar ses on each side of it; underneath the choir is a crypt

Lintel at Montceaux-l'Etoile

of exactly similar shape, very rare in Burgundy but which excavations in 1926 have proved to have existed also at Charlieu and in the Church of Saint-Fortunat.

There is certainly a close relationship between Charlieu and Anzy-le-Duc, not only in the plans of the churches, but also in the style of decoration; it is, however, difficult to establish whether Charlieu served as model for Anzy or whether both were built at the same time. Anzy certainly has a nave with a groined vault and direct lighting and could therefore be considered an offshoot of the Burgundian churches, of which Vézelay is the most famous example. Some archaeologists wonder whether the monks of Saint-Martin in Autun, by adopting a distinctive style of building at Anzy, were not trying to show their independence of Cluny. However that may be, this church is remarkable for its luxuriant decoration both inside and outside. Inside, in addition to the rather unusual Lombardan bands of colour round the apse, are the interesting capitals of the transept and the arches communicating with the cho numbers of small human figures, often bearded, sq and deeply carved, are seen side by side with eagles w outstretched wings, lions and other animals. It has be thought that they are representations of deadly s (Lust, Anger), or of the rivers of Paradise, or j humorous conceptions. The twenty-six capitals in nave are in the same vein, with the same types of hum figures with big heads and slender bodies, but perh somewhat more alive. On the outside, on the muc mutilated doorway is a representation of the Ascensic in the tympanum, Christ in an almond-shaped nimb is supported by two angels; on the lintel, Christ surrounded by the Apostles. Another doorway, de cated to the Virgin Mary, patroness of the church, w moved to a museum in Paray-le-Monial, where it w rebuilt. Finally, above the transept crossing, an octago bell-tower rises in three storeys, similar to that Cluny, having twin window openings flanked by

ies of small arches. The pretty ochre patina of this ll-tower, together with the rose-coloured mortar in ich the long stones of the outside walls are embedded, ve a particularly attractive aspect to this monument. nother representation of the Ascension is to be found the doorway of the nearby Church of Montceaux-toile, to the east of the Loire and slightly further rth, but there the scene is carved, with great freedom expression, in a single stone block, serving both as mpanum and lintel, without any intervening fillet. rist, in an oval nimbus, is lifted gracefully towards sky by two angels with wings outstretched while low, looking at or pointing towards the scene, are rteen small figures, among which may be distin-ished the Virgin and St Peter carrying an enormous y. This church dates from the first half of the twelfth ntury and has a barrel-roof without transverse arches, d a half-domed apse.

★ ★ ★

At the top of the bend of the Loire, at the junction with the Arroux, lies Digoin. Formerly fortified, the town suffered during the fifteenth century from the squabbles between Armagnacs and Burgundians and, in the sixteenth century from the Wars of Religion. One of the leaders of the League was besieged there in July 1593 and was burnt alive in the 'tower' in which he had shut himself up. Today, Digoin is a centre of canal navigation, being the outlet for the seventy-mile-long Centre canal joining the Loire basin to that of the Rhône, while a canal carried over a bridge gives access to the Roanne–Digoin canal. Edged with high poplars, the Centre canal climbs up the valley of the Bourbince, a tributary of the Arroux, and then runs down towards Chalons-sur-Saône by way of the Dheune and the Thalie. The Bourbince rises in the small lake of Montchanin on the plateau between the Loire and the Saône, and its lower reaches flow past Paray-le-Monial in the 'Golden Valley', one of the most popular places of pilgrimage in

France. At this ancient site, a first Benedictine monastery was built in 973 at the top of a nearby hill; at the end of the tenth century, however, after being handed over to the monks of Cluny, the priory was transferred to the place where the church now stands. It was consecrated in 1004, but Abbot Hugh, a native of Semur-en-Brionnais, started its reconstruction, which was still incomplete at the time of his death in 1109. In the course of the Middle Ages the priory experienced numerous vicissitudes, and abbots such as Jean de Bourbon and Jacques d'Amboise did their best to remove all trace of it.

The church is a faithful replica, on a smaller scale, of the great Church of Cluny; it consists of a rather short nave of three bays with side aisles, a very projecting transept, and a choir ending in an apse surrounded by an elegant ambulatory with three chapels radiating from it. At the front of the church is a narthex, the last remnant of the church consecrated in 1004, while the chapel above contains a museum of dressed stones. The nave and the transept arms have barrel-roofs with transverse arches, the aisles and ambulatory have ribbed vaults, while over the transept crossing rises an octagonal dome on squinches. There are typically Cluniac, fluted pilasters at different heights in the nave. The east end is more majestic than the nave as the result of skilful workmanship and decoration. Finally, the vault of the apse carries a superb fifteenth-century fresco made during the abbacy of Jean de Bourbon, which was brought to light again only in 1935.

Paray-le-Monial is especially famous for the pilgrimages which owe their origin to visions which appeared to a great mystic in 1673 and 1689 in the Visitandine convent, namely Marguerite-Marie Alacoque, a nati of the Charollais. She died in 1689, but the cult of t Sacred Heart began only during the Restoration wi the beatification of this Visitandine nun in 1864; t first great pilgrimage took place in 1873. The chap known as 'Chapel of the Visions', with its multitude red lamps, was completely restored and redecorated the nineteenth century.

The town hall is housed in a handsome Renaissan edifice, built between 1525 and 1528 by a wealthy whol sale merchant; its huge façade is decorated wi medallions.

From Digoin, as far as Diou, the Loire flows in wi meanders with numerous villages on wooded hi along the right bank, below which pass both road a railway, while the plain on the left bank allows t lateral Loire canal, a continuation of the Roann Digoin canal, constructed between 1822 and 1837, run almost in a straight line. At Diou a very narro gorge forces canal, road and railway to run clo together.

The whole region south of the wide bend made b the Loire between Pouilly-sous-Charlieu and Diou is continuation of the plain of Roanne; to the west are t last foothills of the Madeleine mountains, spreadi around the tiled roofs of the houses of Donjon a terminating in the look-out point of Puy-Sain Ambroise. From that spot one can see over rich ag cultural lands with large, widely spaced farms, while the north an immense panorama has the Morvan mas as backdrop. Although this region used to be part of t Bourbonnais, Burgundian influence nevertheless ma

Following pages:
Town Hall at Paray-le-Monial

View from Puy-Saint-Ambroise, looking towards the north

itself felt. Thus, the small twelfth-century Church of Neuilly-en-Donjon has a richly carved west door with a tympanum portraying the Adoration of the Magi: the Virgin, seated on a high chair and showing her child to the Magi who are bearing gifts, is surrounded by trumpet-blowing angels; all these outsize personages are carried on the backs of two monsters. From left to right, the lintel portrays Adam and Eve and the Serpent, and next to them the Last Supper. This beautiful piece of sculpture has a clear connection with the church doorways in the region of Autun. The springers of the arches are decorated with palm and acanthus leaves such as may also be seen in the porch of Charlieu.

To the west, this region is limited by the valley of the Besbre, a tributary of the Loire which rises in the Bois-Noir massif; it flows at the foot of Châtel-Montagne with its beautiful Auvergne-style church, runs past La Palisse, the former capital of the Bourbonnais, and winds slowly through a fairly wide valley of rich meadows, both slopes of which provide a setting for many a stately home. Some of these were no doubt damaged in the English Wars, particularly in 1363, and also during the Wars of Religion, for example Puyfol and Chavroches; the last named was in the thirteenth century the domain of the powerful counts of Nevers. Nevertheless, most of these buildings are still inhabited and in an excellent state of preservation. The Château of Jaligny, situated at the point where the road from Roanne to Moulins crosses the river, is certainly the most important of this series of châteaux. It is an imposing fortress, with massive round towers at the corners connected with living quarters which the skill of Renaissance architects made more habitable by addition of decorated dormer windows at the level the sharply sloping attic roofs. The spiral staircase the château is roofed with a radiating vault. Moul bands emphasize the three storeys of the house as wel those of the towers, giving an air of simple elegance the whole. This domain, in which the owners still li is surrounded by beautiful gardens stretching to Besbre river, embellished with fifteenth-cent statuary. During the high Middle Ages, Jaligny belong to owners on the other side of the Loire; in 12 Isabelle of Châtillon-en-Bazois brought it as a dow to Robert, Dauphin of Auvergne, sixth son of Louis; his grandson Guichard, who successfully resis the English in 1363, became cup-bearer to Charles In the sixteenth century, the château was the home Françoise de l'Espinasse and her husband, G d'Amboise, who are responsible for the dorn windows and other openings. Later, Jaligny passed in the ownership of the family of Chabannes de Lapalis

A little upstream, on the other bank of the Besb stands the powerful fortress of Vieux-Chambord, square outlines dominated on the south side by a qu rangular, thirteenth-century keep, whose top is streng ened by turrets corbelled out at the corners; narr stairs are cut into the thickness of the walls. On the ri side, a three-storeyed group of living quarters, forme fortified, connects the keep with another tower; wi mullioned windows over stone benches were opened the fifteenth century to light the interior, which c tains monumental fireplaces. In this case, too,

ìteau is surrounded by a large park. Vieux-Chambord ; remained the property of the same family since the rteenth century; in 1276 the Bishop of Laon, William Jaligny, gave it to Jean Champropin and in 1514 this nily was confirmed in their rights by Anne of Beaujeu, fe of Duke Peter II of Bourbon.

Downstream, on the same bank of the Besbre, two ìteaux of almost the same epoch catch the eye: auvoir and Toury. Behind an old, dry moat a high wer topped by a small lantern looks down on the com-ct mass of Beauvoir. The latter is typical of the fortified vellings of the thirteenth and fourteenth centuries cupied around 1367 by bands of Englishmen who d them as bases for pillaging and holding for ransom idents of the surrounding countryside; legend has it t in one of the towers, today destroyed, was a pit led 'Hell' where prisoners who could not or would t pay a ransom were thrown into a fire. Duke Louis II of Bourbon undertook to dislodge such undesirable guests and seized the place after a siege of eleven days. In the fifteenth century, the rich family of La Fin became the owners of Beauvoir: Jean de La Fin was chamberlain to Charles VII. His son Antoine, *maître d'hôtel* to Dukes Jean II and Pierre II of Bourbon, gave the château its present appearance: wide, mullioned windows open on to flowerbeds and lawns bordered with trimmed yew trees; inside, adjoining halls with pointed vaults, are rooms with coffered ceilings and pendants. Beauvoir belonged to the same family of La Fin until 1606 when Jacques, the last owner, was murdered in Paris, having been very much in favour with Catherine of Medici and especially with Margaret of Valois. Since then Beauvoir has had many changes of masters, but it has survived intact down to the present day.

The rosy granite stones of Toury – according to another legend it was built by a fairy – rising in the middle

Château of Beauvoir

Entrance to the Château of Toury ▶

of the calm Bourbonnais give it a less severe aspect than Beauvoir. It consists of a many-sided wall flanked by round towers and surrounded by moats with at least some water in them; the entrance passes under a high square tower, topped with machicolations between two small pepper-pot turrets; the drawbridge has been replaced by a stone bridge. Inside, the living quarters with their wide windows abut on the enclosing wall, along which runs a parapet walk connecting all the towers. Toury, or Thory, is a very ancient fief; in 1184, Rodolphe de Thory made a donation to the Abbey of Sept-Fons, nearby in the valley of the Loire; about 1410, Guicharde, daughter of Guyot de Thory, whose tombstone is preserved under the porch, married Jean de l'Espinasse; in 1501, her great-grandson Jean de Thory sold the property to Charles Soreau, nephew of Agnes Sorel. For the last two centuries this beautiful dwelling has not changed hands.

After flowing past the township of Dompierre and before running into the Loire, the Besbre runs close to the Cistercian Abbey of Sept-Fons where, in 1663, Eustache de Beaufort started reforming the dissolute ways of the monks. From Diou to Decize the Loire has on its left bank, which is still paralleled by the lateral canal, a rather flat region of heathland containing many pools in the process of drying out; it constitutes the Sologne district of the Bourbonnais. Here the Lo flows under the road from Dijon to Moulins which, r far from the right bank, passes through the importa spa of Bourbon Lancy, already well known in Rom days, and where Madame de Sévigné arrived in 1667 f treatment of her rheumatism. Built on a high hill affor ing a lovely view over the valley, this old city has u usual charm, thanks to its ramparts, its Eperon gatewa its clock-tower and its intelligently preserved wood houses. A little way outside the town an old Cluni priory, founded in 1030 and today a museum, contai some interesting capitals reminiscent of elevent century Nivernais carvings. Then Decize appears on island, with its ring of ramparts not yet visible; on t left bank rises an abrupt escarpment crowned by t ruins of a château of the dukes of Nevers. A little dow stream, a new centre of population has grown up in fro of Saint-Léger-des-Vignes, at the junction with t valley of the Aron; along the latter runs the Nivern canal, planned as far back as the reign of Louis XIII, though the final decision to build it was made only 10 August 1784. Work on it started immediately, but was not finished until 1842. It is the southernmost of t three canals joining the Loire and the Seine. Havi crossed the watershed, it runs down towards Auxer alongside the Yonne.

The Nièvre at Villemenant

The geographer Roger Dion holds that it is at Deciz where the rocks of the edge of the Parisian basin rea the surface, that one passes from 'the wild Loire of t mountains and of the Bourbonnais, winding throu more or less deserted country, to the more civiliz Loire of towns, châteaux and bridges'. Between Deci and Nevers the Loire flows through the great perpend cular faults which break up the southern Morvan, th creating hard limestone promontories alternating wi loops floored with river alluvium. The hills on the rig bank, still mostly wooded, began to be used for breedi livestock in the second half of the thirteenth centur Charollais cattle were introduced here from the Brio nais and then spread all over the country between t Loire and the Allier, the high grounds of which overlo the formidable Château of Chevenon. This squa fourteenth-century, three-storeyed structure is crown with machicolations and flanked by four sturdy towe the principal gate, with its long turrets, is reminiscent the postern at the Château of Vincennes, but here the is neither moat nor drawbridge. In the sixteenth ce tury the lands and the Château of Chevenon belong to Captain François Girard de Chevenon, who was bitter enemy of the Protestants; when the Calvinists Nevers tried to claim freedom of conscience, the recor relate that 'the soldiers housed at Chevenon descend upon them like vultures to fight them and make the abjure the Reformation'.

Coming from Chevenon to Nevers along the rig bank of the river one can, from the end of the bridg take in the whole magnificent view of Nevers spread o in a semicircle on a limestone hill at the apex of a bend

ne Loire. The outline of the high cathedral, the pointed
oofs of the ducal palace, churches and chapels look over
he slate-roofed, gabled houses crowding along narrow,
vinding streets which often end in stairways. The streets
unning up towards the cramped plateau, the site of the
ld town of Nevers, have deliciously archaic names like
treet of the Four Sons of Aymon, Street of Beautiful
pectacles, Street of the Four Winds, Monkey Street, or
ames recalling the crafts formerly practised there: Hill
f the Pottery-Makers, Streets of the Coppersmiths, the
archment-Makers, the Butchers, and Sailors' Quai.
Nevers is in fact a very old city: in Roman days it marked
ne limit of the territory of the Aedui, a people trusted by
Caesar, who kept in this camp his stores, the army funds,
is horses and the hostages taken from other Gaulish
ibes; but the Aedui defected during the big national
prising of 52 BC, massacring the Roman garrison and
urning the town; traces of the old Roman wall can
ill be seen behind the ducal palace. In Clovis' day
Nevers already had its bishop, and excavations carried
ut in recent years under the choir of the cathedral have
vealed the foundations of a sixth-century octagonal
aptistry containing a round font, and six apses radiating
om the centre. The first counts of Nevers appeared in
e tenth century, and the title became hereditary in the
eventh century. In 1063, Count William I built, out-
de the town, the Church of Saint-Etienne, noteworthy
r its purity of style, which bears witness to influences
om the Auvergne and Burgundy. Consecrated in
97 by Yves of Chartres, it became the church of a
uniac priory after being given by William to Abbot
ugh. Saint-Etienne was a stage on the pilgrimage

Beamed house at Bourbon Lancy

Veather-vane
t Anzy-le-Duc

Floods
near Nevers

Château of Cheve

route to Saint James of Compostella. Despite the disappearance during the Revolution of the central tower and the two bell-towers of the façade, it is one of the best-preserved Romanesque buildings in France.

In 1194 Count Pierre de Courtenay, a great benefactor of the city, circled it with ramparts and granted a communal charter; a large part of the twelfth-century wall with its towers still survives in a lovely setting of gardens. In the fourteenth century, when the county was in the hands of the dukes of Burgundy, and subsequently of the House of Clèves, new fortifications were added to those of the previous century, principally the Croux gateway, a remarkable example of military architecture. Begun in 1394 and finished in 1398, it consists of a square tower with two corner buttresses supporting tourelles joined by a machicolated gallery, the whole being roofed with flat tiles; the work was done by a master-builder of Nevers under the direction of Odenet Gendrat and Jean de la Forest.

Inside the walls, work on the building of the cathedral started in the eleventh century and was still going on in the sixteenth. The cathedral came through the centuries without too much damage until the terrible bombardment of 16 July 1944 which destroyed the dome of the east apse and part of the nave; vast repair works, now happily completed, were needed to restore the cathedral. The building contains one very rare feature, namely two apses, a Romanesque one at the west end, preceded by a transept, and a Gothic one at the east end. A half-dome with a twelfth-century fresco covers the Romanesque choir, and the latter rises on thirteen steps over a crypt built in 1028, with ribbed vaults borne on four heavy

pillars. In the thirteenth century a pointed vault
built over the transept which until then had not b
vaulted; between the crossing and the transept a
two big twin arches, formerly supporting the scaffo
ing, meet in the middle on a high, free-standing colur
The fourteenth-century Gothic choir, originally b
over the foundations of the old thirteenth-century ch
and destroyed by fire in 1308, consists of four bays e
ing in a pentagonal apse; high windows and eleg
latticework let in plenty of light; the chapels surrou
ing the choir were much damaged, but it has been p
sible to reconstruct them with the original stones. T
thirteenth-century nave in the Burgundian style, c
necting the two choirs, is flanked by two aisles hav
fifteenth-century chapels along their sides; the bases
the small columns of the triforium running round
nave are decorated with curious caryatid figures in st
naïve poses, representing yokels, burgesses and p
grims; the final touch is provided by a tall square tov
rising over the transept crossing. The fourteen
century sub-basement has little ornament, but the t
higher levels present a riot of balustrades, pinnacles a
gargoyles, with a wealth of large statues portraying
Patriarchs, the Prophets, the Apostles, the Saints, et
these storeys were built by Bishop Jean Bohier betwe
1509 and 1528.

It was a little later, in January 1539, that Ki
François I raised the counts of Nevers to the rank
dukes and peers of France in the person of François
Clèves; in 1566, after the death of her brothers, Henrie
de Clèves became Duchess of Nevers and took
duchy into the family of the Gonzagas of Mantua

The fortified gateway of Croux at Nevers

View of Bec d'Allier

her marriage to Louis de Gonzaga, whom François I soon made Governor of Champagne. The duchy stayed for barely a century in the possession of the Gonzaga family because in 1659 Charles III sold it with all his lands in France to Cardinal Mazarin, who bequeathed it in his will to his nephew Mancini; the Mancini family kept it until the Revolution.

Nevers owes much to the family of Clèves as well as to the Gonzagas, who completed the elegant ducal palace begun in 1475 by Count Jean de Clamecy, by adding, to the Gothic building with its massive round towers, features presaging the approach of the Renaissance, in particular the stairway in the middle of the façade. It rises inside a small tower lighted by high, square windows placed spirally; the bases of the windows are carved with scenes in low relief depicting the legendary origins of the House of Clèves and, in par cular, the tale of the Knight of the Swan, which serv as inspiration for Wagner; damaged during the Revol tion, the carvings were repaired in the nineteen century by the sculptor François Jouffroy. In the care ing light of the sun, the beautiful stone of the façade tak on warm golden tints. This château, sometimes d cribed as the 'First Château of the Loire' because of construction date, is the first of the series of sumptuo buildings along the Loire in its course after Nevers.

Nevers also owes to the Gonzagas the establishme of its potteries. Louis de Gonzaga brought from Ita workmen skilled in the art of ceramics, glass-maki and enamelling, who established themselves in the low part of the town around 'Potters Hill' and even had th own church, Saint-Genest, built in the twelfth centu

ow a garage. The production of ceramics continued in ll swing until the Revolution; at the beginning, it was tirely in the pure Italian tradition, but in the eighteenth ntury different styles were adopted; during the Revo-tion, ceramics with patriotic designs were made, to-ther with what were called 'wedding' plates. This dustry is now declining, although one factory founded 1648 is still in production in the quarter of the town here the earliest ceramic factories existed. Today, her industries have started up around the town of evers, although the centre of activity has left the quays the Loire, from which manufactured goods formerly gan their journey, and is now concentrated near the ation and the main road.

From the seventeenth century onwards the whole ivernais region enjoyed great prosperity, thanks to its forges. For centuries there had been many small forges which owed their origin to tiny deposits of iron-ore, as is shown by many of the local names; but it was due to the encouragement of Colbert that a tin factory was created in 1635 at Coulange on the Nièvre. Then, in 1636, a forge was installed at Guérigny, also on the Nièvre, very near the manor of Villemenant with its curious crown of wooden panels; in 1637 another forge appeared at Imphy, several miles upstream from Nevers. In the eighteenth century, the Guérigny forges de-veloped rapidly under the encouragement of the Baron de la Chaussade and became the most important in France at that time. The supplies which they provided for the American fleet certainly helped that country to achieve its independence. They were bought in 1781 by Louis XVI for the nation, and today, with their administrative offices lodged in the eighteenth-century château, they are still in production under the name of National Forges of the Chaussade. The forges at Imphy nowadays concentrate on the production of special steel; it was there that the July column (in the Place de la Bastille) was made and many of the parts composing the Eiffel Tower were cast and worked. Finally, since 1818, below the Bec d'Allier, the centre of Fourchambault has grown up around its forges between the Loire and the road to Pouges-les-Eaux. Thus, this whole region, despite the exhaustion of the iron-ore deposits, is still an important industrial zone.

Between Nevers and Fourchambault the Loire flows in a wide loop in the middle of which, close to the little village of Bec d'Allier, it is joined by its tributary, the Allier, coming from the south. In order to see the whole of the immense panorama around this junction of rivers, extending from the Loire valley towards Germigny and Cours-sur-Barre – formerly known as Cours-sur-Loire – as far as the high ground around Magny-Cours between the Loire and the Allier, one must leave Nevers and go west to the centre of the promontory in the middle of the loop of the Loire, at a point close to the little township of Marzy with its beautiful Romanesque bell-tower. This well-favoured region, where many a Nivernais has built his country house, is covered wi vines – particularly around the hamlet of Sain Baudière with its Montepins vineyard – and is remin scent of the Touraine. Rich pasturelands stocked wi Nivernais cattle slope gently down to a Loire of cal aspect. Opposite, over the Allier, its bed encumber with islands and sandbanks, three bridges carry t road, the railway and a canal, providing communicati between the Nivernais and Berry. A romantic histori describes the junction of the two rivers in these term 'After having avoided each other for a long time order to avert comparison, the Allier at last bows to t invincible will of Nature and reluctantly throws its into the Loire, like a noble heiress forced into a marria by which she loses her illustrious name.' One has oft wondered why the lower course of the Loire has n been called the Allier. Certainly, of the two streams t Loire has a bigger average flow of water than its trib tary and is longer, but it seems rather that the questi was decided on historical grounds, since confirmed b custom: the high valley of the Loire has been, from t time of the first human migrations, the most direct a the shortest route for travel between Provence and t shores of the Mediterranean, on the one hand, and t plains of the Parisian basin, on the other.

Central staircase in the pala
of the dukes of Neve

Following page
looking towards Sancer

The Loire of the Abbeys and Châteaux

low the Bec d'Allier, the Loire flows almost parallel two north–south faults, cutting into the east flank of e Massif Central; if it had continued to flow in the same rection as before, it could have joined the Seine some-here near Paris; the two river basins are separated by ly a low watershed and because of this canals joining e two rivers have been easy to construct. Between iare and Orléans, however, the waters of the Loire rn first to the northwest and then, at Orléans, squarely f to west-southwest; in the Miocene geological riod they flowed into the Faluns sea which at that ne extended as far as Blois.

In its long course as far as Anjou, flowing in a bed clut-red with islands often overgrown with vegetation, and ith frequently shifting sandbanks, the Loire flows ostly along the foot of rocky hills overlooking one or e other of its banks, on which most of the centres population are built. On the other hand, the valley ovides an easy outlet for flood waters into a lateral pression, which threatens at times to take the place the principal river bed. The sudden and often sastrous floods of the Loire are a permanent affliction r the local people and authorities, who have for cen-ries been trying to protect the low-lying land by eans of dikes or levees and to regulate the excessive riations of the water level.

This wide valley is generally known as the 'Vale of e Loire', but the designation 'Vales of the Loire' would better because each section has a different appearance; e Vale of Saint-Benoît or the Vale of Orléans do not semble at any point the Vale of Touraine or the Vale Anjou. The abbeys and châteaux built in this natural framework are evidence of a refined civilization, and the valley has been the stage for many of the principal events of French history, for example Joan of Arc's ride. But it has also known the sadness of wars, invasions and foreign occupations with their attendant train of destruction, pillage and massacre.

The first place truly entitled to be regarded as a town of the Vales of the Loire is La Charité, where can be found, to quote Roger Dion, 'the precise, peaceful arrangement of the classical Loire landscapes'. It is from the left bank that one can best see the whole of this city, built on the slope of a hill, where old houses with high chimneys crowd around the beautiful Romanesque bell-towers and buildings of the ancient monastery. A suburb has grown up on an island joined to both banks by ancient stone bridges, several arches of which were destroyed in 1940 and 1944. According to tradition, the first monastery was founded about 700 by St Loup and subsequently destroyed and reconstructed several times; but the history of La Charité really begins only during the eleventh century, when the Bishop of Auxerre and the Count of Nevers in 1507 made a gift to Abbot Hugh of Cluny of everything they possessed in this place. At this time work was started on a monastery so magni-ficent that it earned the title of 'Eldest Daughter of Cluny'. The construction of the church must have been sufficiently advanced in 1107 for Pope Paschal II to come and consecrate it. Thereafter the monastery de-veloped considerably; donations poured in, and in the twelfth century it was one of the richest monasteries in Europe, with two hundred monks in residence. Many priories attached themselves to it not only in France but

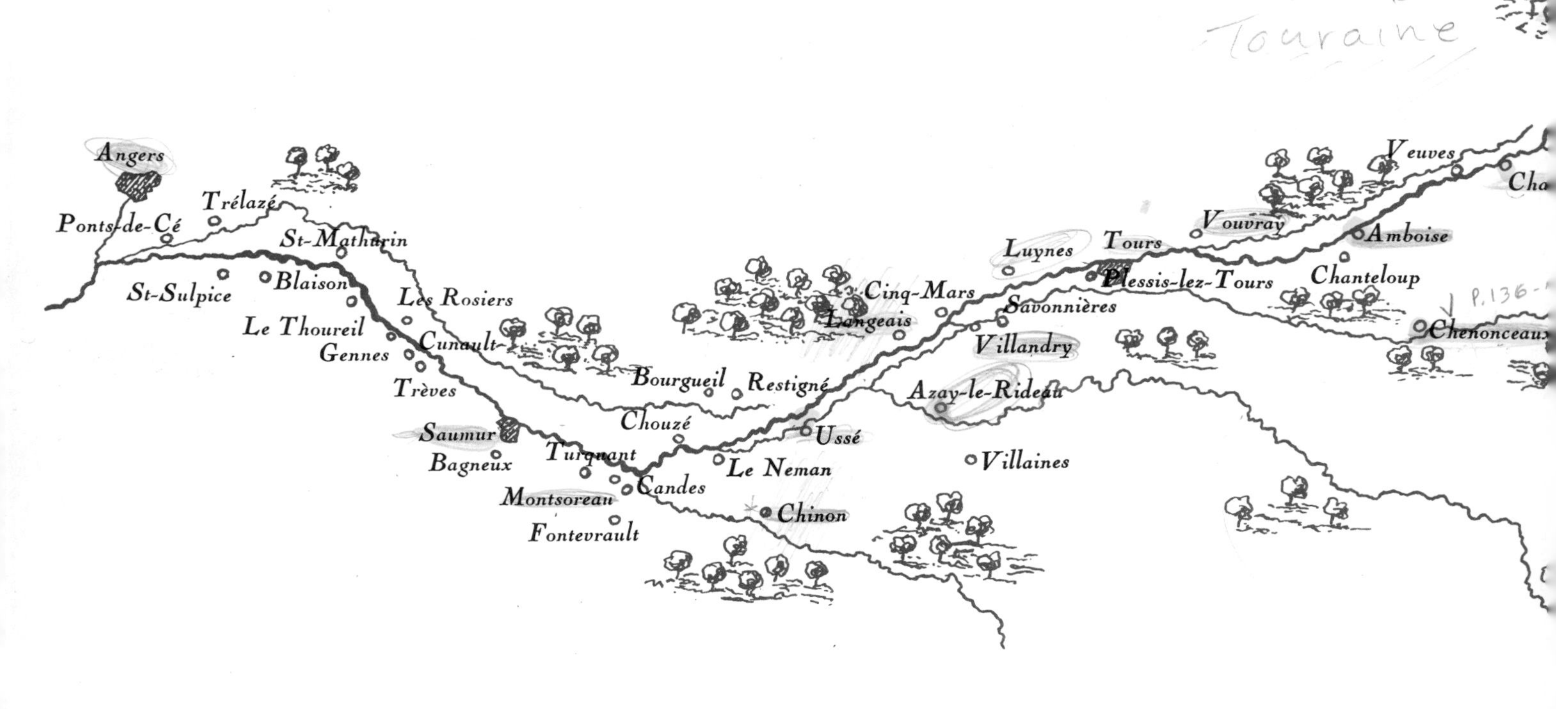

throughout Europe as far as Constantinople. In order of precedence, its prior came immediately after the Grand Prior of Cluny. The houses which rose around the scaffolding of the monastery were protected from 1081 by an encircling wall, some traces of which remain together with the Cuffy Tower; but the ramparts were not sufficient to defend the place against assault and pillage, although Joan of Arc, coming here to fight the Burgundians after the coronation of King Charles, failed to take it. After taking Saint-Pierre-le-Moutier by assault, she came in December 1429 to besiege La Charité, then defended by an adventurer named Ferrin Gressart; but after one month her troops, poorly arme and lacking provisions, were forced by the cold to li the siege. In the sixteenth century, the Wars of Religic were for La Charité nothing but a long sequence of ma sacre, pillaging and destruction, by Catholics as well Huguenots; the magnificent monastery church suffere particularly during these wars.

The Church of Sainte-Croix-Notre-Dame, com pleted in the second half of the twelfth century, was t largest in France after Cluny and could hold five tho

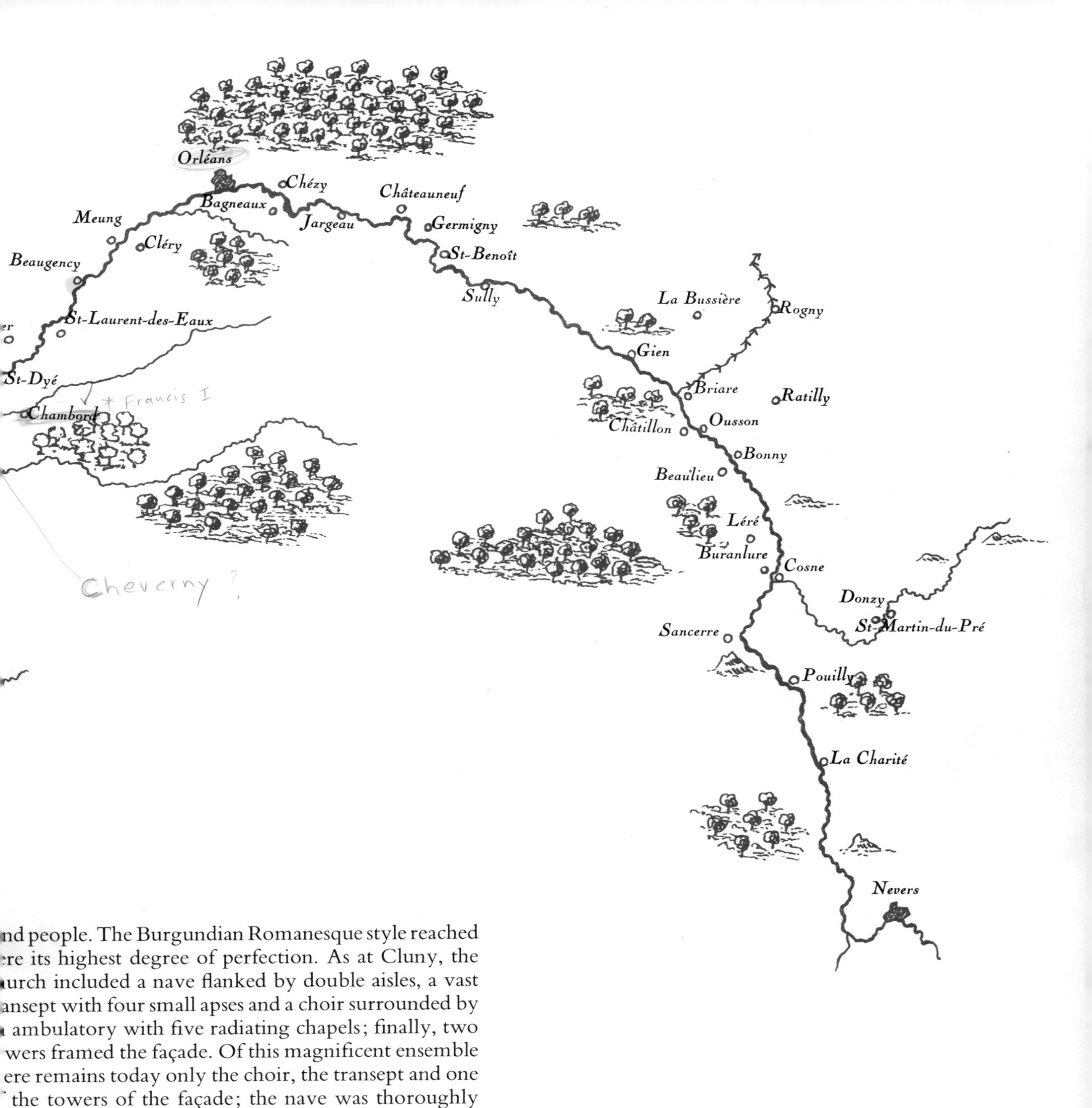

nd people. The Burgundian Romanesque style reached ·re its highest degree of perfection. As at Cluny, the ·urch included a nave flanked by double aisles, a vast ansept with four small apses and a choir surrounded by · ambulatory with five radiating chapels; finally, two wers framed the façade. Of this magnificent ensemble ere remains today only the choir, the transept and one ` the towers of the façade; the nave was thoroughly cked and burnt by the Huguenots in 1559, but four ·ys were preserved and rebuilt in the eighteenth ntury.

The Loire from Nevers to Angers

La Charité:
steeply sloping roofs
in the town

La Charité:
details of sculpture
on the ancient abbey

In the choir with its pointed cradle roof, the carvings
n the capitals above the high columns of the hemicycle
ortray a great variety of subjects: foliage or monsters or
imals (elephants, dromedaries). A small dome on
uinches covers the transept crossing and the octagonal
ock-tower is embellished with large statues. The
terior decoration of the remarkable east end and of
e transept is in no way inferior to that of the inside.
he tympana and the lintels of the doorways which
rmerly framed the west front, now separated from the
ve, have been preserved, one in its original place while
e other has been moved to the south arm of the tran-
pt. With their subtle rendering of draperies, the carv-
gs are evidence of great concern for accuracy allied to
rare delicacy of expression. On one doorway is carved
e Glorification of the Virgin together with the Annunciation, the Visitation and the Nativity; on the other, Christ is shown standing in an almond-shaped nimbus between large figures of old men beneath an Adoration of the Magi and a Presentation in the Temple. The architecture of La Charité had great influence throughout the region of the Yonne, especially at Auxerre.

The monastery precinct extended to the north of the church and its buildings, although reconstructed in the seventeenth and eighteenth centuries, have nevertheless preserved some elements from the fifteenth century, notably the old abbot's house.

After La Charité the vale gets broader. On the left bank a flat, wooded region stretches to the approaches of Sancerre, bordered on the one hand by the Berry Champagne with its copses, meadows and fields, and

La Charité:
detail of the church porch

Backwater of the Loir
at Pouill

on the other by the line of the river with its willow-covered islands. On the right bank, undulating hills, to which in the twelfth century the monks of La Charité introduced the culture of the vine, today produce an excellent wine, notably at Mesves, where a twelfth-century tithe barn stands and, above all, at Pouilly-sur-Loire as well as in more remote regions such as Les Loges, Le Bouchot and Saint-Adelain. Chasselas grapes are also an important item of commerce. This wine-growing country is the twin of the vineyards of Sancerre, stretching along the left bank immediately contiguous to the town of that name which is built a short distance from the river on a hill of siliceous sandstone. All around, a multitude of small properties cultivated with scrupulous care by cheerful wine-growers produce a quality wine, light and of delicate flavour but somewhat treacherous. These wines, already famous in the thirteenth century, were in great demand in Paris. The region of Sancerre also produces small cheeses of goats' milk known as *chavignols*, the pottery moulds for which are made locally.

The hill of Sancerre is the only really high ground along the course of the Loire until it reaches the sea; its position, at the top of a bend of the Loire at the extremity of the Berry region and facing the Nivernais, made it one of the key cities of central France. Surrounded by an oval enclosure comprising nine towers, and with its château on top of the hill, of which a round fifteenth-century keep known as the Fiefs Tower survives, Sancerre was one of the strongest fortified places of the Middle Ages. In the ninth century Thibaut le Tricheur, Count of Blois, took possession of it and from the middle of the eleventh century Sancerre re-mained in the hands of the counts of Champagne, al-though the town was sometimes claimed by the count of Nevers. Sancerre was of some importance during th Hundred Years' War; a large force trying to gain pos-session of the town in 1364 was destroyed and in 143 the English were defeated in its vicinity.

In the sixteenth century, Sancerre embraced th Protestant religion and played a considerable part in th Wars of Religion. The townsfolk harried and pillage shipping on the river. In 1560, the town was unsuccess-fully attacked several times by the Catholics and in 156 it was besieged, again without success, for five months after the massacre of St Bartholomew the town refuse to open its gates to the royal troops. In 1573, Sancerr had to undergo one of the fiercest sieges of the entir sixteenth century; surrounded by the troops of L Châtre and without artillery, it resisted for eight month (from 3 January to 19 August); the lack of food becam so acute that the citizens were reduced to eating th parchment of their old charters and manuscripts afte softening it in water. Finally, in 1621, the Prince c Condé took the place and razed the ramparts to th ground. In the tenth century, a priory existed in th town, a dependency of the Abbey of Fleury-sur-Loir the present-day Saint-Benoît; it was destroyed durin the Wars of Religion and the monks had to take refug in the mother abbey and, in 1561, in Orléans. At the foc of the hill, the village of Saint-Satur served as river po for the products of the region.

Between Sancerre and Cosne the valley narrow forming a sort of corridor in which the river, the later

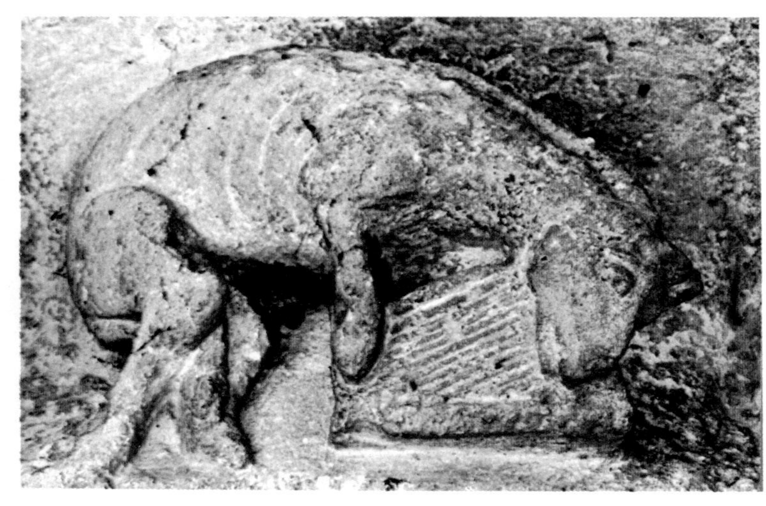

Donkey musician in the church of Saint-Aignan at Cosne

The Loire above Sancerre

Following pages:
general view of Sancerre

A goat at Chavignol

nal, the road and the railway run close together. Along
: right bank is a series of well-cultivated knolls where
: population lives in widely separated hamlets. Further
ck is the Donzois, a region composed of Jurassic
ateaux abutting on dense forests along the western side
which flows the Nohain. Before entering the Loire at
osne, this river flows past Donzy, the ancient capital
a barony whose lords were vassals of the bishops of
uxerre and played an important part in the Nivernais
ring the thirteenth century when Henry VI of Donzy
came Count of Nevers; an ancient keep rises above
is township on an isolated rock. In one of the suburbs
as a priory, which became attached to Cluny in 1109
d grew very prosperous as the result of numerous
nations from the bishops of Auxerre. Of the priory
urch, damaged by the wars of the thirteenth century
d burnt by the Protestants in 1569, a doorway survives
hose tympanum is one of the masterpieces of Cluniac
ulpture. It portrays the Virgin in Majesty seated under
canopy in the Byzantine style, the infant Jesus on her
ees; an angel with outstretched wings to the left
vings a censer, and on the right stands a large human
gure which could be the prophet Isaiah. The influence
Brionne can be felt in the modelling of the draperies
d the angel's wings. Donzy, in fact, at one time
longed to the lords of Semur.

Cosne-sur-Loire, which under the name of 'Condate'
as mentioned in the Itinerary of Antoninus, belonged
the sixth century to the bishops of Auxerre; in the
nth century, one of them donated part of the revenues
the domain of Cosne to the canons of his cathedral and
dered a château to be built at that spot as protection

Château of Buranlure, near Cosne

against Norman incursions. The domain, however, was of such importance that it could not but be coveted by others and, notably, the counts of Nevers; after many fights during the early twelfth century count and bishop concluded an agreement in 1157. Like all the rest of the valley, Cosne suffered from the Hundred Years' War and the Wars of Religion, and its old fortifications disappeared only during the reign of Louis XIV.

As far back as in the eleventh century the monastery of La Charité founded a priory at Cosne, of which the Church of Saint-Aignan remains, despite remodelling in the twelfth century and partial burning in 1737. The west doorway is without a tympanum, thus relating the building to the architecture of the Loire valley. Its double, semicircular vaults are embellished with sm scenes, each of a different subject, carved on the twent five voussoirs composing the archivolt; in the centre Christ in Majesty is seen between a donor and a mon surrounded by the symbols of the Evangelists and sor fantastic monsters and animals, including a donk playing a musical instrument. Inside, the hemicycle the choir is well lit by five windows and is rich in scul ture; the capitals of the high columns framing the wi dows portray unusual subjects such as heads of cat-li animals shown upside-down and figures of men faci each other and holding animal heads. Outside, the bli arcades decorating the east end call to mind those La Charité.

Angel carved on
the tympanum of
Saint-Martin-du-Pré,
Donzy

Château of Assay

The canal bridge at Briare

A long island in front of Cosne divides the Loire into vo arms, spanned by two stone bridges; downstream, her wooded islands have emerged in the course of the ges. On the left side of the valley, which widens until it aches the narrows of Ousson, low-lying, waterlogged nd stretches to the lateral canal; few people live there ecause flood waters have often risen to levels threaten-g the villages and their inhabitants. Nevertheless, close the canal on this plain, we find the important urteenth-century Château of Buranlure, completely ncircled by moats whose waters reflect the big towers f the wall; a gateway, formerly protected by a draw-ridge, opens under a massive square tower. Small in-abited localities such as Léré, Belleville, Beaulieu, have ught the protection of the other side of the canal.

On the right bank, where the Loire flows very close to the foot of the hills, townships with their churches and their châteaux crowd into the mouths of small lateral valleys, such as La-Celle-sur-Loire, Neuvy-sur-Loire, Bonny-sur-Loire. Behind them, a monotonous table-land extends as far as Loing-le-Puisaye, composed of hard soils (clay, silex) with numerous pools, grazed by flocks of sheep. There are few villages but some châteaux, for example the old Château of Assay (thirteenth century) with its massive walls and a gate-tower topped by machicolations between two tourelles; or the Château of Ratilly (thirteenth century), which has kept its corner towers intact as well as two big towers flanking the gateway, now used as a workshop for the production of fine pottery.

Lateral canal
above Châtillon

It is near Ousson that the Loire picks up the flinty pebbles which it will deposit along the whole of its remaining course. At Châtillon, a mile or so downstream, the lateral canal of the Loire, constructed between 1822 and 1837, formerly ended by running into the bed of the river itself; but in order to avoid the dangers inherent in this arrangement, the canal was continued to Saint-Firmin, opposite Briare, and a canal-bridge, begun in 1890, and the largest construction of its kind, now serves as a junction with the Briare canal. The Briare canal itself was the first in Europe to negotiate two slopes. Work on it was started under the supervision of Sully in 1604, interrupted during the political troubles at the time of Louis XIII's minority, restarted in 1624, and finally finished in 1638. From Briare it climbs the valley of the Trézée and then descends the valley of the Loing which it follows as far as Buges; there it joins the Orléans canal to form the Loing canal, joining the Seine downstream from Moret. At Rogny, on the ridge between the Loire and the Seine, a very curious construction was carried out between 1604 and 1606 on Sully's orders, namely a monumental stairway of seven locks, built with the idea of conducting the waters of the Trézée into the valley. It is now abandoned and has been replaced by seven locks much further apart. The Briare canal formerly carried a lot of traffic between the Mediterranean Sea and the Parisian basin, but today there is very little.

After Briare the Loire bends towards Gien, passing Saint-Brisson on the left, in former times a powerful barony of the Berry. This township has kept intact a fortress dating from the thirteenth and fifteenth centuries. Then, on the right bank, Gien appears in the shadow of its elegant château. This very ancient tow suffered cruelly from bombardment in June 1940; t town centre with its many old houses has now be tastefully reconstructed. Gien was the property of t barons of Donzy, under the overlordship of the Bisho of Auxerre; in 1179, Henri de Donzy sold the fief to Ki Philippe Auguste, who freed the townsfolk from duties of vassalage to the bishops of Auxerre. It w separated from the Crown on several occasions, bei given in appanage or as a jointure, or placed in paw The old feudal château was reconstructed by Anne Beaujeu, daughter of Louis XI and Countess of Gi from 1494 to 1500. Gien takes pride in being the site the oldest fair in France; started in 581 by Gontram, Ki of Orléans, it is still held every year in the month March. The town became famous thanks to its potteri During the Middle Ages, it was important as a point passage between Burgundy and Berry; Joan of A crossed the Loire at this spot in 1429 on her way fro Vaucouleurs to Chinon; both she and Charles VII al passed through at the end of June on their way Rheims for the coronation. Today, the lovely ston and-brick château, where kings often stayed, has be cured of the wounds received during the war and h been, since 1952, a museum of sporting guns ar falconry. No other place could have been more appr priate for this, given the proximity of the famous gan reserves of the Sologne and the Gâtinais. In the museu are works by the great animal painter Alexandr François Desportes, also a fine collection of guns.

Besides shooting, fishing is very important in t Loire. It is therefore appropriate that since 1962

Château of Ratilly

Following pages: general view of Gien

nuseum of fishing has been installed at La Bussière, north of Gien, in a seventeenth-century château surrounded by moats and a park designed by Le Nôtre; here one may follow the whole history of fishing since prehistoric times.

After Gien the banks of the Loire take on a different ook; the river starts to wander through the clays and ands of the Sologne depression between the Sologne to he south and, to the north, the Orléans Gâtinais and forest; it will not regain its classical, straight appearance until after Orléans. The Sologne, stretching south to the Cher and westward to Cléry, used to be a very poor country with soft contours, covered with heathlands and dotted with pools. Drainage works and reafforestation carried out in the nineteenth century have turned it into a relatively prosperous region, with birch and pine woods, some agriculture and pasturelands for stock-farming. In autumn it becomes a paradise for sportsmen, many of them members of shooting clubs whose game preserves are strictly protected; hare, rabbit, snipe, pheasant and partridge abound.

The Orléans forest, a wooded mass of some 125,000 acres on soil of granitic sands similar to that of the Sologne, stretches in a vast crescent between the Gâtinais, with its heathland and heather, to the wheatfields of the Beauce. This region, with its deep forests, was the home of the Carnute tribe and was mentioned by Caesar; but the forest areas have dwindled more and more in the course of the centuries as a result of wasteful customs of the inhabitants, clearing operations by the monks and devastations wrought by the wars of the fourteenth and sixteenth centuries; in the nineteenth century the government began reclaiming this forest, planting pines, oaks, birches and hornbeams; many pools still exist, such as the Etang du Moulin and the Etang de l'Evêque north of Saint-Fargeau; the clearings are fairly well cultivated and large stock-breeding farms are to be found on the southern edge of the forest. The vale is covered with small market and fruit gardens, but the vineyards are tending to disappear.

The nearer one gets to Orléans, the more one finds in each town, each château, each abbey of the valley reminders and evidence of great events in French history. First of all, there is the imposing Château of Sully from which Henry IV's minister took his name; situated on the left bank, this ancient lordship, first mentioned in the ninth century, passed into the possession of the family of the counts of Chartres at the beginning of the twelfth century and thereafter into the suzerainty of the bishops of Orléans; finally, in 1381, it became the property of the de la Trémoille family by the marriage of Marie de Sully with Guy de la Trémoille. One of the latter's descendants, George, at first a partisan of the Burgundian cause, made his submission in November 1418. An early château was then in existence; built no doubt in the fourteenth century and later remodelled, it is the rectangular building facing the Loire, with four round corner towers known as the 'keep'; the magnificent framework of chestnut wood dates from 1363 and was the work of Thévenin Foucher, one of Sully's artisans. Charles VII and Joan of Arc stopped here on their way to the coronation at Rheims and it was also here that Joan spent a month in the spring of 1340 before starting on her last ride, which ended with her capture at

Compiègne on 23 May. During the Wars of Religion, both the château and the town were captured and pillaged by Protestants and Catholics alike. In 1602, the window of Claude de la Trémoille (who had been converted to Protestantism and become one of the lieutenants of Henry of Navarre), sold the domain of Sully for 120,000 *livres* to Maximilien of Béthune, Baron of Rogny and Grand Master of the French artillery, who at once started to work on the château at the same time as he studied the possibility of joining the basins of the Loire and the Seine by a navigable canal. In 1606 the king elevated the Lord of Sully to the rank of duke and peer, thus depriving the bishops of Orléans of their feudal rights, an event which subsequently gave rise to many lawsuits.

After the death of Henry IV, his old minister retired to the château where he lived in sumptuous, almost royal state, with a retinue of gentlemen, pages, esquires, Swiss guards and French guards whom he inspected every day. Continuing the work of embellishment on the site of the chapel of the old manor, dedicated to St Ithier, he completed the big round tower known as the tower of Béthune, whose foundation stone had been laid in 1605. As protection against the Loire floods a solid wall was built in the park and the château then appeared as an irregular square, with the new buildings joining the big tower to the old château. While the work was in progress, Sully dictated daily to his four secretaries the text of his book *Economies Royales,* which was printed in the Béthune tower at Sully in 1638 by Jacques Bouquet, a master-printer from Auxerre. Three years later Sully died in the Château of Villebon; his mortal remains were rediscovered in 1883 after many vicissitudes and are now at rest in a small oratory of the chapel.

The successors of the great Sully continued the work of embellishment and, during the seventeenth and eighteenth centuries, maintained a court where writers and men of wit were welcomed. Duke Maximilien-Henri, who married the daughter of Madame Guyon, had the twenty-two-year-old Voltaire as guest at the château during summer and autumn of 1716 and again in the summer of 1719. A theatre was installed in the first storey of the old château where Voltaire staged the *Nuits Galantes* and *Artemise* in which the daughter of an officer of the Sully Bailiff's Court made her debut; after unsuccessful attempts at theatrical rôles under Voltaire's direction, she later married the French ambassador in London.

During the Second World War, the town of Sully was much damaged, first in June 1940 by Italian air attacks and German artillery and in 1944 by Allied bombardment. Two-thirds of the town was destroyed. Like Gien, Sully has been a crossing-place of the Loire since ancient times; a very old route from the north passed over the Loire here on a bridge mentioned in 1364 which disappeared in the last years of the sixteenth century but was rebuilt in the nineteenth century. It was destroyed on 19 June 1940, at the same time as the village of Saint-Père on the right bank, rebuilt in 1942, destroyed again in 1944, and finally reconstructed in 1947.

Below Sully, in a bend of the Loire, are the village and Abbey of Saint-Benoît-sur-Loire, built on a hill above flood level. This place, where the abbey church has stood for eight centuries, was formerly known as Fleury

e locks at Rogny

Following pages:
Château of Sully-sur-Loire

cording to some historians it was the 'umbilicus' of Gauls, where druids from all the tribes used to meet h year. However this may be, we know that about year 630 the Abbot of Saint-Aignan d'Orléans, odebod by name, having failed to impose the Benetine Rule on his monastery, decided to found an bey on lands at Fleury which King Clovis II had given him in exchange for the domain of Attigny. Some rs later, about 703, Abbot Mommole took the venturous decision to send one of his monks, named gulfe, to Monte Cassino in the south of Italy to find remains of St Benedict in the ruins of the abbey founded by him but deserted by his monks after its destruction by the Lombards. The prosperity of the Fleury monastery, which subsequently took the name of Saint Benedict on the Loire, was based on its possession of these important relics. Pilgrims began to arrive there in the eighth century and the later Merovingian kings made big donations. Two churches were built prior to the magnificent abbey church of the eleventh and twelfth centuries.

As far back as the ninth century, in the time of Charlemagne, Saint-Benoît became an important intellectual centre. Abbot Theodolph, who was at the same

time Bishop of Orléans and played a big part in the Carolingian Renaissance, set up schools which during the reign of Charles the Bald had up to five thousand pupils; in the scriptorium a magnificent collection of manuscripts was gathered by the copyist monks and illuminators. Unfortunately, this abbey, like so many others in the valley of the Loire, was damaged, particularly in 985, by raiding Norsemen who periodically sailed up the river from the sea. After re-establishment of the Benedictine Rule in 988, the schools became active again. Abbot Abbon, who had spent two years in England, brought students from across the English Channel. A future archbishop of Canterbury was a pupil, as well as Gerbert, who had previously studied science in Arab institutions in Spain and who became the first French pope under the name of Silvester II. During the abbacy of Gauzlin, a natural son of Hugh Capet, who became abbot in 1004, the influence of the schools under the leadership of a monk of great erudition, named Isambard, spread far and wide. Gauzlin enriched the treasury with items in ivory and gold plate; he sent to Italy for artists to decorate the two churches which still existed at that time but were to be destroyed in the fire of 1026.

The holy relics were miraculously preserved through all these disasters and Abbot William, who ruled the abbey from 1067 to 1080, started to rebuild the Church of Notre-Dame with help from King Philip I, who had a particular veneration for this abbey. The work started at the beginning of the twelfth century with the choir, the transept and the bell-tower porch, and it was sufficiently advanced for the bishops of Orléans and Auxerre to arrive there on 12 March 1108 to consecrate tw altars in the presence of the future Louis VI. Sever months later Philip I died and was buried in the cho as he had desired. A stone slab supported by four lio today marks the site of his tomb, which was redi covered during excavations in 1958–59. Then the r construction of the nave was started. Many importa personages came to visit the church, including Po Paschal in 1103; a Provincial Council was held there 1110 and in 1131 Pope Innocent II came for its co secration. It was not, however, completed until 12 when it must have had about the same aspect as we s today. Under the direction of Raoul Tortaire the schoo continued to flourish during the twelfth century, part cularly the school for illuminators; literary clerics wro mystery plays. The abbey was so rich that Louis V borrowed from it the money he needed for his crusad

A noteworthy event in the fifteenth century was t visit of Joan of Arc who, after freeing Orléans, came urge Charles VII to have himself crowned at Rheims. the year 1486 the abbey was put *in commendam*; certa abbots, such as Chancellor Duprat, were not w received by the monks, and François I ordered the be tower porch destroyed in punishment, an order whi was happily only partially carried out. Another abb the brother of Admiral Coligny, became a Protesta and plundered the abbey treasury. Finally, in 16 Richelieu introduced the reforms of Saint-Maur.

At the Revolution, the abbey buildings were s and demolished. The partially ruined church w abandoned and might have disappeared altogether b luckily, it was classified as a monument in 1835, and t

Château of Saint-Brisson

:ensive restoration work carried out over more than
undred years has returned it more or less to its original
te. In 1947, a group of monks from the Monastery
Pierre-qui-Vire began reconstructing the abbey
ildings.

The church is one of the most remarkable Roman-
ue buildings in France. The narthex, dating possibly
m the last third of the eleventh century, consists of a
ge square tower, its lower part forming a porch with
all naves roofed over by groined vaults borne on
ssive pillars topped by fifty-four capitals carved with
iage or scenes of great beauty. On the first storey
re was a room built to the same plan, and above that a
rey with machicolations and a square tower, but these were demolished in the sixteenth century. There is a lovely doorway on the north side of the nave, dating from the first quarter of the thirteenth century; the door is flanked on each side by three caryatid columns representing prophets; the story of St Benedict is portrayed with great realism on the lintel; in the tympanum above, a handsome Christ making the gesture of blessing is flanked by the four Evangelists and their symbols.

The transept, as wide and as high as the central nave, has two small apses in each of its arms. The very deep choir, surrounded by an ambulatory with four radiating chapels, is in two parts: a straight bit where the old floor slabs brought from Italy by Cardinal Duprat are again in position and the flanking columns topped by magnificently carved capitals (Adam and Eve in the earthly Paradise, Abraham's sacrifice, the Temptation of St Benedict, etc.); the second part is a hemicycle following the shape of the crypt, with pillars spreading out around the big central shrine containing the relics of St Benedict.

A few miles from Saint-Benoît there stood, in Charlemagne's time, the palace of one of the liveliest intelligences of his era, Theodolph the Goth, who was born in Spain and was doubtless of Spanish origin; Charlemagne sent for him to help with the revival of science and literature. Poet, theologian and statesman, he became Abbot of Saint-Benoît-sur-Loire about 799; on land belonging to the abbey he built a sumptuous villa, which is known to us only from descriptions in his poems. Accused later of plotting against the emperor, he was banished in 818 and his villa confiscated. Charles the Bald must have stayed in it in 854 and 855.

The chapel of this villa, of which contemporaries speak with admiration, fortunately has come down to us after a long period of neglect, in the course of which the interior was whitewashed in the eighteenth century; in the nineteenth century, on the initiative of Mérimée, this monument, unique in France for its design and decoration, was restored. It was built to a rectangular plan with a central dome and four apses of which three survive, the east apse having two smaller apses on either side. The interior must have been entirely covered with mosaics of which only the big mosaic, with its unusual design, in the vault of the east apse remains: on a gold-enamelled, blue background the Ark of the Covenant, decorated with cherubs, is flanked by two big archangels whose figures hug the curvature of the dome, while above them appears the Hand of God. The mosaic bea a Latin inscription reading in translation: 'See here tl Holy Oracle and the Cherubim, and note how Goc Testament shines forth. As you contemplate the things and seek by your prayers to appease the wrath the Lord of the Thunders, I beseech you to include your devotions the name of Theodolphus.' It was on thought, though erroneously, that this mosaic had be brought from Ravenna, and it now seems certain th it was made locally, perhaps by mosaicists who h come to the abbey to work.

Situated very close to Germigny, Châteauneuf-su Loire is an ancient domain which Philip I in the eleven century turned into one of his favourite residenc Taken by the English in 1428 and ruined during t Wars of Religion, Châteauneuf became in the seve teenth century the property of Phélypeaux de Vrillière, Secretary of State to Louis XIV, who bu there a magnificent château which was almost entire demolished in 1803; only some of the service quart survived. A large part of the town, including the Chur of Saint-Martial, was destroyed during the Seco World War, but the funerary monument of Phélypea escaped; Paul Vitry is of the opinion that it is probab the work of an Italian artist, doubtless a pupil of Berni he says, 'It explodes with dramatic action'.

* * *

The porch, Abbey
Saint-Benoît-sur-Lo

After Saint-Benoît, the Loire flows over a bed of limestone torn by many fissures, where its waters are engulfed and follow an underground course as far as the source of the Loiret. There has always been the fear that during heavy floods the Loire might abandon its normal course and flow into the Loiret depression, thus ceasing to run by the quays of Orléans, and because of this danger protective works have been undertaken; since 1412 Jargeau has had its embankments and levees and at the beginning of the sixteenth century a dike, twenty-five miles long, was built from the hamlet of Bouteille on the left bank, almost opposite Saint-Benoît, to the Abbey of Saint-Mesmin-de-Micy, close to the junction with the Loiret.

Jargeau, once an important centre of barge navigation, is famous particularly for the bloody victory won there by Joan of Arc on 12 June 1429, after she had liberated Orléans; the fortified township was taken by assault and Joan was wounded by an arrow. The wedding of Louis XI's daughter Anne to Pierre de Beaujeu took place in the old church here, consecrated in 1154, but destroyed by the Huguenots. Jargeau becomes the site each year in November of a curious 'Chestnut Fair'.

Throughout this part of the valley, as far as Orléans, Joan of Arc is vividly remembered. A little downstream from Jargeau, on the right bank, Joan's mother Isabelle Romée came to live with her youngest son, Pierre de Lys, in the small farm of Bagneaux from which she tried to prod the religious authorities into rehabilitating her daughter; two years before her death she had the joy of hearing at Orléans, on the 21 July 1456 the solemn proclamation of the rehabilitation decree. Then there are the stages of Joan's approach towards besiege Orléans. She came from the south; on 28 April 1429 sh crossed the Loire at Chécy and on 29 April she entere Orléans with her convoy of supplies. At Saint-Loup, little further along, a small monument stands to remin us that at that point on the river bank stood the fort c Saint-Loup, which Joan carried by assault on 4 Ma 1429 in her first encounter with the English. On the nex day but one, 6 May, she took the Augustin bastion finally, on 7 May, the bridgehead on the left bank of th Loire, the Tourelles fort, fell into French hands afte furious fighting. On 8 May the English army raised th siege and beat a retreat.

Since its foundation this city has played an outstanc ing part in the political, religious, economic an intellectual life of France, to which the valley of th Loire with its easy communications made an importar contribution. About 56 BC, Julius Caesar occupie 'Cenabum', an important town in the country of th Carnutes – one of the principal tribes of independer Gaul – where a port was already in existence; but i 52 BC 'Cenabum', which had given the signal for a bi national uprising, was burnt and pillaged and its peop sold into slavery. Long afterwards, perhaps in the thir century, a new city was built on the ruins of the ol protected by a solid, quadrangular enceinte, which cam to be known as 'Civitas Aurelianum' (whence Orléans A Gallo-Roman civilization then developed throughou the region; the Loire boatmen provided river transpo between Roanne and its stores of goods from beyon the mountains and the commercial ports along th middle Loire. In the fourth century Christianity can

Joan of Arc,
from a tapestry
in Orléans museum

the valley and its bishops were destined to become ry influential. In the fifth century, Attila and his Huns scended from the north and laid siege to Orléans; it as Bishop Anianus (St Aignan) who took charge of e defence and threw the invaders back in June 451 th the aid of the troops of Aëtius. In 463 the city also pelled attacks by the Visigoths, who had come from quitaine. In 498 Clovis took the town and made it one his residences; in 511 he held there the first Church ouncil of Northern Gaul. In the same year, when the st division of the kingdom took place among the sons Clovis, the kingdom of Orléans emerged and was stowed on Clodomir; a short time later, in 561, ontran also took the title of King of Orléans. The arolingians took an interest in Orléans; Charlemagne couraged its intellectual renaissance by bringing in shop Theodolph, who founded schools at Sainte-roix and Saint-Aignan; Charles the Bald had himself owned in the cathedral. However, Norsemen pushed eir raids as far as the town and in 865 all churches tside the walls were sacked. When Hugh Capet, ount of Orléans and Paris, was elected King of France July 967, he incorporated Orléans in the royal mains; his successors often resided in the district; in 08, Louis the Fat had himself crowned at Orléans. ter, the domain was made into a duchy for the nefit of members of the royal family, but it was united with the Crown in 1499 by Louis XII. Separated ain during the reign of Louis XIII, the duchy con-ued to exist until the Revolution.

In the course of the centuries Orléans suffered not only the Hundred Years' War but also during the Wars of Religion and even those of the Fronde; the wars of the nineteenth and twentieth centuries also caused much damage. Orléans was occupied by the Prussians in 1815. They returned there in 1870, sacking its suburbs; in June 1940, Orléans was bombarded by the Germans and in 1943 and 1944 by the Americans. More than six hundred houses were destroyed, and the lovely eighteenth-century bridge was damaged. But while its strategic position at an unavoidable point of passage between north and south has often brought violence to Orléans, the town has also often known periods of great prosperity, thanks to this same position. Its easy river and land communications have made it an important centre of transit and commercial exchanges.

Since the high Middle Ages, big fairs have been held at Orléans; merchants from Flanders stopped there on their way to Spain; Jewish and Lombard moneylenders plied their trade under the jurisdiction of the bishop. All kinds of goods were to be found there: cloth from the north, leather, furs, ironwork from Berry and the Nivernais, spices from the East. The powerful 'Community of the Merchants of the River Loire and Its Tributaries' who were the successors to the 'Loire Navigators', established its headquarters at Orléans where delegates of the local associations of boatmen and merchants used to meet in general assembly. One of the tasks of this organization was to oppose the innumerable tolls levied by the local lords and also to contribute to the expense of maintaining and marking the navigable channel.

Despite the difficulties occasioned by the irregularities of navigation in the Loire, traffic was intense during the seventeenth century. Madame de Sévigné, who often used this means of travel when visiting her daughter at Les Rochers, recorded the touting habits of the boatmen on the quays of Orléans: 'Hardly had we arrived here than twenty boatmen were around us'; in 1663, La Fontaine marvelled at the movement of boats 'driven by sails': 'it seems to me that I am seeing a small version of the port of Constantinople'. Regular river services started only in the eighteenth century; the water-buses took four and a half days from Orléans to Nantes, but light boats, or *cabanes*, could do the trip from Orléans to Saumur in sixteen hours under favourable conditions. In the nineteenth century, river transport began to decline, although it had seemed that the steamship would bring new life to navigation on the river. Various companies, such as 'Les Inexplosibles' ('The Non-Explosives') and 'L'Etincelle' ('The Spark') were founded between 1840 and 1843, at the same time as the first railways appeared in the valley of the Loire; in 1843 the Paris–Orléans line was opened and in 1846 it was extended to Tours and in 1851 to Nantes. In spite of the ensuing price war, travellers and goods forsook the river. Since then there have been many proposals for reviving navigation on the river: the lateral canal project suggested at the start of the twentieth century by a company called 'La Loire Navigable', which disappeared in 1914; studies and projects by the 'National Association for the Study of the Community of the Loire and its Tributaries (ANECLA)', a company formed in Orléans in 1967; and a plan for utilizing a new conveyance, the naviplane, capable of a speed of 250 miles per hour on an air cushion.

Yet another waterway is of interest to Orléan namely the Orléans Canal, built in the seventeent century between the Loire and Seine basins. In 1679 concession for it was granted to the Duke of Orléans fo the transport of wood to Paris, and the canal w completed in 1692. It was confiscated in 1791 an bought by the State in 1860; its present traffic is ve modest.

If navigation on the middle reach of the Loire h practically come to an end, movement by land along th valley has always been very easy. The Romans improve the old Celtic roads converging on Orléans; in th thirteenth century the *Guide des Pèlerins*, for the use pilgrims going to Saint James of Compostella, mentio the road from Orléans to Tours along the left bank far as Blois and after that along the right bank; the roa along the right bank between Orléans and Blois w opened only after the Marquise de Pompadour acquire Ménars. In the *Guide des Chemins de France* (1552) it stated that the road runs along a dike; dikes of eart were indeed built at certain points, from the elevent century on, to protect the riverside population fro floods. An edict by Charles the Bald in 821 mentio the dikes of the Loire, and in the fifteenth centur Louis XI caused the existing embankments to b heightened. In 1571 a superintendent of levees w specially charged with responsibility for the 'main tenance of the said works throughout all the length o the course of the Loire'. By the eve of the Revolution seemed that both banks of the middle course of th river were sufficiently protected; nevertheless, durin the nineteenth and twentieth centuries catastroph

The Loire at Beaulieu

›ods occurred, notably in 1856, 1866 and 1920; as a
medy for the future the ANECLA has suggested
nstruction of vast low-level overflow reservoirs.
Orléans has also been an intellectual centre almost
ntinually since the Carolingian renaissance, and
rticularly in the eleventh and twelfth centuries, when
schools attracted students not only from France, but
.o from England and Italy. Eminent professors taught
etoric there and, from the twelfth century on, canon
v and Roman law, the teaching of which was for-
lden in Paris; French as well as Latin was used in the
ssrooms. On 2 January 1305 a Bull of Pope
ement VI, who had been a student at Orléans,
thorized the schools to group themselves into a
iversity; in 1312 Philip the Handsome gave his
consent. Squabbles arose frequently between students and citizens, and in 1376 a more violent brawl caused the temporary exodus of the university to Nevers where, as the result of fresh disorders, the townsfolk were provoked into throwing the Master's official 'chair' into the Loire. Back at Orléans the university developed brilliantly, except during the Wars of Religion. At the start of the seventeenth century it was still fairly famous, but the Revocation of the Edict of Nantes brought about the departure of many foreigners. In the eighteenth century, the number of students declined considerably as the result of competition from the universities in Paris and Bourges. Today, Orléans is again becoming a university town, its campus well on the way to completion.

The church at Cléry: Louis XI on his tomb

Only a few buildings have come down to us through the successive destructions to bear witness to the city's glorious past. The Cathedral of the Holy Cross rose at the end of the thirteenth century on the site of two older buildings; it was burnt by the Calvinists in 1568 before it had been completed; reconstruction, begun in 1601, was not completed until 1829; excavations carried out in 1937–38 revealed the remains of three earlier sanctuaries. The twelfth-century Church of Sainte-Euverte was ruined during the siege of 1429, but reconstructed in the fifteenth century. The Church of Saint-Aignan, reconstructed after the same siege, was subsequently damaged by the Protestants who destroyed the nave, but the interesting crypt was fortunately preserved; it was built between 984 and 1029 by Robert the Pious. Houses dating from the Middle Ages are few; the rue Royale was made between 1752 and 1756 but has had to be reconstructed. However, the old Law School Library has survived and is known as the 'Salle des Thèses'; it is a late fifteenth-century square hall with elegant, octagonal columns, now used by a local scientific society.

Orléans today has become the capital of central France, after some competition from Tours. But the fact that it is close to Paris, with which it may soon be connected by a hovertrain, has made it difficult for Orléans to impose itself as a local metropolis despite its flower festivals, despite the 3,500 students in its still-unfinished university and despite its large industrial zone, still not fully developed. It is to be hoped that the policy of regional decentralization may soon allow the town to achieve a status worthy of its historic past.

South of Orléans flows the Loiret, a river which is i fact a resurgence of the waters of the Loire reappearin out of two springs, the 'Bouillon' and the 'Abîme situated in the middle of a splendid park. Countr houses of the people of Orléans line the banks of th tributary which, after passing through the village Olivet in its lovely setting, runs into the Loire at the en of its eight-mile course; the junction occurs close to th site of the former Abbey of Micy, an importa institution founded by St Mesmin during Clovis' lif time, from which many hermits emerged, like St Av who went to Orléans and St Liphard who settled Meung.

The town of Cléry, famous for its basilica, lies some distance from the Loire. The origin of th sanctuary goes back to 1280, when a statue of the Virg was discovered buried in the ground and soon becan the object of a cult. The local feudal lord as well Philip the Handsome enlarged the chapel, but it w sacked and destroyed in 1428 by English soldiers und the command of the Earl of Salisbury. After the liber tion of Orléans, a new edifice arose due to the generosi of Charles VII and of Dunois, the faithful companion Joan of Arc. Louis XI, while still Dauphin, vowed spec devotion to Notre-Dame de Cléry and, in 1467, ga to the church the status of Chapel Royal, at the sa time announcing his wish to be buried there. He died 30 August 1473, after having bought Cléry from Dunois family earlier the same year, and a monume was erected over his tomb. During his lifetime he h moreover, asked several people – particularly Jeh Fouquet and Michel Colombe – to submit plans for t

The church at Cléry: sculpture detail

ıonument. He finally reached an agreement with ;onrad of Cologne, a goldsmith living at Tours, and aurent Wrine, gunsmith and metal caster. This first, ilt-bronze statue, portraying the king kneeling, was ıelted down in 1561 by the Huguenots, who also estroyed the glass window and burnt the statue of the irgin dating from 1280. Not until the seventeenth ntury, in 1622, was a new funerary monument ected; the work of Michel Bourdin, a local sculptor, was destroyed at the Revolution. Finally, after the discovery of the royal tomb in 1889, containing the ortal remains of the king and his wife, a statue of the ng kneeling was again placed there. The heart of harles VII reposes almost opposite.

A number of very ornate chapels have been added to is magnificent Flamboyant church with its vast size d harmonious proportions. The Longueville family apel was built between 1464 and 1468 and under its tricate vaulted roof the courageous Dunois lies buried ith members of his family; the Villequier chapel, above ıich is a small room with a fireplace, is the burial-ıce of André de Villequier, the complaisant husband Antoinette de Seignelay, who succeeded Agnes Sorel Charles VII's favourite; the even more ornate Saint nes chapel was built between 1515 and 1519 by lles de Pont-Briant, Dean of Cléry, and his brother; latter was also employed by Louis XII and François I supervise the work on the Châteaux of Blois and ıambord. It is likely that the future master-masons of ıambord participated in the work of building the last these three chapels; on the other hand, Pont-Briand s once captain of the Château of Loches, whence he could have taken the ideas of cable-moulding and ermine tails, both of which are to be seen in the oratory of Anne of Brittany.

While Cléry is situated in the alluvial plain on the left bank, the little towns of the right bank, such as Meung-sur-Loire and Beaugency with their flower-decked houses, stretch along the limestone slopes of the Beauce bordering the river on that side. In the ninth century a monastery existed at Meung-sur-Loire as well as a school, which was mentioned as far back as 848 as one of the schools for the clergy which owed their inspiration to St Liphard. Meung used to be part of the domains of the bishops of Orléans, who sometimes experienced difficulties with their vassal, the lord of the town; in the twelfth century they were forced to build a protective tower supported by the clock-tower of the the old church and, at the same time, a bridge over the Loire. Then, in the thirteenth century, at a short distance from the new church, they built a château which became their habitual place of residence. It was to this château, occupied alternatively by the French and English during the Hundred Years' War, that the Earl of Salisbury came to die after receiving mortal wounds near Orléans. The town is also connected with a literary event: it was here that Jean de Meung wrote the second half of the *Roman de la Rose*, the most widely read literary work of the Middle Ages. Later, in the eighteenth century, a bishop, Mgr Jarente de la Bruyère, a partisan of Choiseul, was exiled to this place, where he built a luxurious mansion facing the Loire; it was considered a sign of good taste to stop here on one's way to Chanteloup.

Preceding pages:
Orléans

Bridge of Beaugency

Capital in the Church
of Notre-Dame
at Beaugency

Throughout its history, Beaugency has known many
cissitudes. The origin of the local noble family is very
oscure; they could have been vassals of the bishops of
miens. The domain was granted by Hugh Capet to a
rtain Landry but a descendant of the latter sold it back
Philip the Handsome. In the Hundred Years' War
e English took it in 1367 and still held it at the time of
e siege of Orléans. Joan of Arc, however, accompanied
the Duke of Alençon, started out towards Beaugency
ter taking Jargeau and the city very quickly sur-
ndered. Then Count Dunois, the Bastard of Orléans,
ceived the domain as his wife's dowry, but under the
igns of François I and Henri IV it passed through the
nds of many owners before becoming the property
the Duke of Orléans. During the Wars of Religion,
eaugency was more than once occupied by the
alvinists, who pillaged the place. Finally, in 1944,
eaugency was bombarded fourteen times, but the old
rt of the town fortunately escaped.

An example of military architecture, invaluable
spite its state of dilapidation, looks down upon this
arming city. It is an enormous, rectangular construc-
on, which originally consisted of four floors rising
ove a vaulted basement; the lower two storeys were
nnected by straight staircases with barrel-vaults built
to the very thick walls. This imposing keep, which is
metimes known, for no reason at all, as Caesar's
ower, was badly damaged in 1567 by a fire which
stroyed the roof and all the floors; the cause of the
saster was a spark from a fire started by the Protestants
hile sacking the neighbouring abbey. The tower was
ver repaired and was sold during the Revolution.

This keep was part of a complex of fortifications built to protect the Loire crossing, where a bridge has stood since the high Middle Ages. The twenty-two very picturesque arches of the bridge were built, or rebuilt, at different times, notably in the sixteenth century, and were restored after 1945. Beneath some of the arches stood water-mills, and a chapel dedicated to St James rose in the middle of the bridge. Close to the keep, Dunois rebuilt in the fifteenth century an old house with an attractive small tower containing a staircase; it now houses the local museum. Beaugency also has several very quaint old houses, particularly one which now serves as its town hall; this Renaissance construction with its medallion-studded façade, was built about 1526 by the master-builder Charles Viart, who is thought to have worked also at Orléans and Blois. The old Abbey Church of Notre-Dame, erected in the twelfth century, was burnt down by the Protestants in 1567, together with the abbey buildings; the latter were repaired in the eighteenth century.

Beaugency had a dependency in the lordship of Talcy, connected with Mer by the 'Rose Road'. This lordship was acquired on 8 November 1517 by the Florentine merchant, Bernard Salviati, who was related to the Medicis and had established himself in France, where he carried out a number of financial operations on behalf of François I. In 1520 his feudal superior, the Lord of Beaugency, who was at that time Jean d'Orléans, Archbishop of Toulouse, gave him permission to rebuild the château with its 'walls, towers, barbicans, loopholes, machicolations, drawbridges and other items required for the defence of a stronghold'. Talcy, in fact,

Portrait of Madame de Pompadour

as it now exists, still looks like an early sixteenth-century medieval château, with its square, turreted keep topped by a parapet walk; nevertheless, the interior courtyard, with its lovely wellhead under a dome, contains an arcade of four basket arches, revealing burgeoning Italian influence. In addition to the Talcy Conference of 1562, called by Catherine de Medici and the Prince of Condé in an attempt to end the Wars of Religion, the château evokes two memorable events, one literary and the other romantic. Ronsard wrote a poem to Cassandra, a daughter of Bernard Salviati, whom he had met in 1545 at the Château of Blois. Thirty years later, Agrippa d'Aubigné conceived a mad passion for Diana, granddaughter of the same Salviati. The château was acquired by the State in 1933.

As far as Blois, the Loire continues to flow along the line of hills on its right bank, except between Avaray and Montlivault where, on the left bank, it runs past the terrace of Saint-Dyé with its wooded hinterland, very different from the humid Sologne area drained by the Cosson and the Beuvron. This reach of the Loire, which in summer flows sluggishly between sandbanks, lies at the foot of the magnificent gardens of the Château of Ménars, acquired by Madame de Pompadour in 1760. The château itself, begun in 1646, underwent such extensive alterations in the eighteenth century at the hands of the Marchioness and her brother that hardly anything remains of the original edifice; the architects Gabriel and Soufflot worked on the alterations. From the south terrace two majestic ramps run down to flowerbeds in the French style, surrounded by a vast sheet of water, in a setting of greenery. On the north side, the most beautiful avenue of lime trees in the wor calls to mind the picture in which the Marchioness portrayed against a background of greenery.

The region of the 'Châteaux of the Loire' real begins at Ménars. Although not all these buildings a situated on the banks of the river it was in this area tha for nearly two centuries, châteaux were built, readapte or embellished by kings, great officials, royal favourit and substantial citizens, all of whom made valuab contributions to the development of monument architecture. It is curious, however, that anyone stud ing this development when travelling down the vall of the Loire through the Blésois and Touraine, gets t impression of going backwards through histor because the renaissance of Touraine flowered a reached its highest development *after* the court h moved from Chinon downstream towards Blois a Chambord.

In the tenth century, Blois became the capital of county whose power at times extended over parts Touraine, the Dunois and even the Champagne. In t eleventh century, there was already a church at Bloi its interesting crypt was rediscovered in the twentie century and is known as the crypt of Saint-Solenn Thibaud le Tricheur, one of the earliest counts, built keep on the site before 978, which Count Steph encircled with walls at the end of the eleventh centur but no trace of these defensive works remains. This w the period of the feudal wars between the counts Blois and the counts of Anjou, who were also kings

The avenue of lime trees at the Château of Ménars

Gargoyles on
the Château of Blois

England, for the possession of the Touraine; man traces of these struggles can be found, even as far a Saumur and beyond. In the thirteenth and fourteent centuries, another line of counts, of the Châtillon famil held the county of Blois for nearly the whole perioc From that time a great hall – known as the 'Hall of th Estates' because the Estates General met there durin the reign of Louis XIII – has come down to us, as we as the Foix Tower and some thick walls which have bee incorporated in later buildings. In 1391, Guy c Châtillon sold the county to the brother of Kin Charles VI. After the assassination of the latter in 140 and the death of his inconsolable widow in 1408, the son Charles, who became Duke of Orléans and Cour of Blois in addition to being a great French poet, mac the Château of Blois his favourite residence after h return in 1440 from twenty-five years' captivity i England. Little remains of the works carried out by th prince, but they are fortunately known to us fro contemporary plans and drawings.

On the death of Charles VII in 1498, Louis II, born a Blois in 1462, succeeded to the throne under the name c Louis XII and began to renovate the old fortress. H concentrated principally on the east wing, where bric lozenges enliven the walls and the charming doorway embellished with an equestrian statue of the king belo a magnificent canopy, against a blue backgroun covered with golden fleurs-de-lis; the original statu was destroyed in 1792, but was replaced by a copy i 1857. A lovely gallery, with alternating round an square columns, opening on the courtyard, provid evidence of Italian influence, especially in the details c

Staircase in the
François I wing
at the Château of Blois

Typical farm in the Loire valley near Veuves

the decoration. About the same time, the Chapel of Saint-Calais was rebuilt and huge gardens, no longer extant today, were laid out on the north side by Pacello da Mercogliano, a Neapolitan brought from Italy by Charles VIII.

Immediately after becoming king on 1 January 1515, François I, husband of the daughter of Louis XII, Claude, who had been brought up in the Château of Blois, began to extend the work of his predecessors, starting with the northwest wing. The massive thirteenth-century walls and the three towers built against them were completely covered with dressed stone, inside and out; a suite of large rooms with monumental fireplaces was built facing the courtyard; a projecting newel staircase rises in the middle inside an octagonal tower; this part of the building is remarkable for its decoration, borrowed from Renaissance Italy and matching the increasing luxury of the court. Much originality is manifest in the treatment of the north façade, with its two superimposed loggias surmounted by a long gallery featuring picturesque gargoyles. After Queen Claude's death in 1524, and upon his return from the period of captivity which started after the disastrous battle of Pavia in 1525, François I seems to have deserted his residence on the banks of the Loire in favour of Fontainebleau. The last of the Valois kings, Henry II, Charles IX and Henry III, still frequently stayed in the Loire châteaux and used the river for their visits in preference to the land route. It is impossible to speak of this period without mentioning the tragic murder of the Duke of Guise on 23 December 1588 and the death, a few days later, of Catherine de Medici.

Work on the buildings of the Château of Blois di not end with the sixteenth century. Gaston of Orléan brother of Louis XIII, having been granted, in 1626, th county of Blois in appanage, decided to set up h residence there; finding the Gothic château unworthy c his rank, he entrusted to Mansard the job of building château in the classical style in place of the work done i the sixteenth century by Charles of Orléans. The col grandeur of the new buildings is in sharp contrast wit the charming magnificence of the other wings wit which it quite fails to harmonize. After the death c Gaston of Orléans in 1660, the château returned to th Crown; in 1788 Louis XVI ordered it to be sold or, i the absence of any purchaser, to be destroyed. Th building was saved by being used as barracks, but th Army gradually abandoned it and it was finally restore by the Administration of Historical Monuments.

The château suffered little during the Second Worl War, despite the destruction of more than thre hundred houses in the town by German bombardment Among the buildings destroyed by fire were man wooden houses which had been among the town's chi attractions. Fortunately, some lovely Renaissanc mansions survive, such as the Hôtel d'Alluye built b Florimond Robertet, treasurer of the kings of Franc and certain neo-classic buildings like the old episcop palace with its beautiful terraced gardens, built b Gabriel at the beginning of the eighteenth century. Th cathedral, damaged by a hurricane in 1678, was rebui at the end of the seventeenth century. However, Blo possesses one of the most important religious edifices the twentieth century, the Basilica of Notre-Dame-d

Field of maize near Candé

Trinité; built of diamond-pointed cement, its interior coration is in harmony with the architecture. The wn still attracts many visitors today and hopes to ntinue doing so; an immense lake has been created a le upstream on the Loire by a dam, and swimming, ating, and water-skiing have thus been made ailable.

On the left bank of the Loire, in the heart of the ulogne Forest, the counts of Blois, in the twelfth ntury, possessed a hunting lodge in a domain of more n twelve thousand acres. François I chose this lated spot to erect one of the most splendid edifices nceivable in those days, the Château of Chambord. ork on it went on from 1519 to 1524, and again from 27 to 1532; the terraces were finished in 1537, one ar before the king's death, and in 1546 the gilded lead of of the keep was put in place. François I's successors ntinued, and sometimes altered, his work, in particular nen they replaced the flat roofs with mansard roofs. s still doubtful who inspired or invented Chambord; s known that eighteen hundred men worked under direction of master-masons with typically French mes: Jacques Sourdeau, Pierre Neveu and Jacques oqueau; but it is also known that a wooden model for nambord was made by Dominique de Cortone, knamed 'Le Boccador' (Golden Mouth), who, having eviously been at Amboise during the reign of narles VIII, worked at Blois and later drew up plans the town hall in Paris.

The layout of Chambord follows the usual pattern of ench châteaux. On the north side of the large parallogram of the enclosure rises a rectangular edifice between four round towers, simulating the keep of old French fortresses. In the centre is a monumental stairway. Two people can use it simultaneously without meeting, as it consists of two ramps, one above the other.

François I visited Chambord frequently, especially during the last years of his reign, and there, in 1539, he received the Emperor Charles V, who admired the château as 'being the epitome of the achievements of human endeavours'. After the death of François I, the court seldom came to the château, but it must not be forgotten that Louis XIV had staged there, for the first time, two of Molière's plays, *Monsieur de Pourceaugnac* in 1669 and *Le Bourgeois Gentilhomme* in 1670. The château is now owned by the State; in the park there are more than five hundred free-ranging deer.

At an equal distance from Chambord and Blois, beyond the Boulogne and Russy Forests, rises a magnificent residence, the Château of Cheverny. In 1504, war treasurer Jacques Hurault bought the lordship of Cheverny; in 1510, his son Raoul, financial treasurer and a relative, moreover, of Bohier and Berthelot, who were then working as architects in Touraine, built a manor at this place, some elements of which survive in the appurtenances of the existing château. After having been Diane de Poitiers' property for some time, the domain was returned, in 1564, to Philip Hurault, who became Governor of the Orléanais and the Blesois in 1582. It was his son Henry who, in 1634, started the construction of the present château, entrusting the work to a man called Boyer, architect in Blois, and it was a Blois painter, Jean Mosnier, whom he employed to decorate the interior. The construction, however,

Château of Chaumont, looking towards the Loire

would never have been successfully concluded if it had not been for Henry's second wife Gareland Gaillard. During the eighteenth century and the early years of the nineteenth, the château passed through various hands, and suffered from it; for a short time after 1765, Dufort, a marshal of the Diplomatic Corps, made the place habitable again and gave sumptuous parties there; but it was not until 1825 that it passed into the hands of a family of architects, the Vibrays, who have exerted themselves to restore it to its former splendour. This building consists of a rectangular central area flanked by two large square pavilions roofed with domes. It is specially noteworthy, however, for its furniture and the splendid decorative painting on both the ground and first floors; on the latter, in the king's room, hang eight tapestries portraying the Labours of Ulysses, which is the only complete set of such hangings woven in Paris during the seventeenth century to the cartoons of Simon Vouet.

After Blois, the white mass of the Château of Chaumont rises on a talus in the middle of lovely wood Founded at the end of the tenth century by Eudes Count of Blois, this domain was given, about the ye 1026, by Eudes II to his vassal Geldouin, who former owned Saumur in Anjou but which Foulques Nerr Count of Anjou, had just taken away from hir Subsequently, a granddaughter of Geldouin marri Sulpice d'Amboise and Chaumont became the proper of that family and stayed so for five hundred years; the twelfth century, Hugues d'Amboise built a sto keep there. However, when Sulpice II of Amboise sid with the counts of Anjou, Thibault V of Blois to possession of the fortress of Chaumont in 1154 a razed it to the ground. Once again, in 1465, the châtea

General view of the Château of Cheverny

ıich had meanwhile been rebuilt, was demolished by ıler of the king because Pierre d'Amboise had become nember of the League for the Public Good. It was ıin rebuilt, apparently with assistance from the king, t its reconstruction was not finished until the early ırs of the sixteenth century. After the death of nry II in 1560, Catherine de Medici bought Chau-ont, but soon exchanged it for Chenonceaux which longed to Diane de Poitiers. After passing through ıny hands, Chaumont became State property in 1938.

Originally, this château consisted of a square central ırtyard surrounded by buildings on all four sides. molition, in 1740, of the north wing facing the Loire ısiderably increased the attractiveness of this dwelling. e oldest part, the right wing, with its large southwest ver, known as the Amboise Tower, was built tween 1465 and 1475 by Pierre and Charles I of Amboise. It is still a military building where everything has been sacrificed to the needs of defence; the curtain wall, originally containing a few openings, is surmounted by a covered parapet walk with crenellations, loopholes and machicolations; the Amboise Tower is a true keep. The east and south wings were the work of Charles II of Amboise between 1498 and 1510; although the loopholed towers flanking this part of the building make it look like a fortress, it does not seem that the idea was to add to the defences; there are even some bits of decoration to be seen.

★ ★ ★

Following pages:
Château of Chambord

Shortly after leaving Chaumont, the Loire enters Touraine, where the landscape takes on a different appearance. Flowing through the valley parallel to the course of the Loire is the Cisse, a small river split into a number of separate streams overhung by willow trees; since the end of the fifteenth century new crops have been cultivated here alongside the traditional ones. Here the sand carried by the stream from the river terraces of the Bourbonnais forms soil, which, if not very fertile, is at least very easy to work and suitable for quick-growing crops. Agriculture is the principal economic activity in this Touraine section of the valley where grazing lands alternate with orchards, small vegetable plots and large fields of maize around well-separated farms.

Below Blois, the valley bottom no longer runs through flint-bearing chalk but through the tufa which provides the beautiful white building stone for the houses of Touraine; the ease with which it can be worked has since the remotest antiquity fostered the creation of cave-dwellings, which can be found as far as Ponts-de-Cé and beyond. Cellars have been dug into this stone by the vine-growers, whose crops cover the hill slopes.

The Château of Amboise, on a site formerly used as a point of lookout and defence for a passage over the Loire, stands on a chalky escarpment on the right bank, at the tip of a spur overlooking the junction of the Loire and the Amasse. A château was first built at this place by Hugh I of Amboise, who had managed to unite three pre-existing lordships under his control, and the domain of Amboise remained in his family until King Charles VII confiscated it from Louis of Amboise in 1431. It was some time the property of George de la Trémoille, b returned to the Crown on his death in 1446. Charles V and especially Louis XI, who often stayed here befo retiring to Plessis-les-Tours, had a certain amount work done on the château, of which only some tow of the enceinte and the containing walls rema Charles VIII was born in this château in 1470; after marriage to Anne of Brittany in 1491, he came to li here and at once started work on the wing facing t Loire, which has undergone many alterations since the Of this king's other constructions only the Saint-Bla Chapel has survived; it is now known as the Sai Hubert Chapel, and was begun about 1493 and co pleted on the king's return from his expedition Naples. The chapel now stands by itself on the châte terrace vertically above the enceinte wall; it is delicat decorated, particularly its interior, roofed with ogival vault with both liernes and tiercerons. The lin above the double door of the façade bears, on the le a carving depicting a legend of St Christopher and, the right, a representation of one of the visions of Hubert; this very colourful but rather pedantical precise work of art recalls the carved wooden retab of Flemish sculptors, and it is known that artists from t north, such as Cusin of Utrecht, were working in t château at that time. The inside walls of the chapel a abundantly decorated; one frieze portrays a tall, nak Eve facing the Serpent.

Influences from a different source can be perceived the two massive towers, which are the most origir parts of the château. The Hurtault Tower on the sou

e Saint-Hubert chapel, Amboise:
: on the external cornice

The Saint-Hubert chapel, Amboise:
a detail of the façade

e, looking over the valley of the Amasse, was
mpleted at the end of the reign of Charles VIII; the
ıer, the Minimes Tower on the side facing the Loire,
s not finished until the reign of François I; under
:ir ogival vault rise two spiral ramps up which one
y ride on horseback or be carried in a litter; beside
listic, typically French themes there are many details
carving which derive from a new fount of typically
ramontane inspiration; Italian artists, like Jérôme
:herot, were in fact living at Amboise.
Charles VIII called on the services of Pacello da
:rcogliano to design an Italian garden to the east of
: terrace; and Louis XII, during whose reign the work
Amboise was rather abandoned in favour of Blois,
ther embellished this terrace by the construction of a
all gallery leading to a door surmounted by his
blem, a porcupine. François I paid several visits to
nboise and attracted a notable guest, Leonardo da
nci; he also received the Emperor Charles V there in
39. During the reign of François II, Amboise was the
ne of the horrible massacres which followed the
nboise conspiracy, and one of the balconies of the
ade is still known as the Conspirators' Balcony.
Abandoned in the sixteenth century and poorly main-
ned during the following centuries, Amboise was, in
: reign of Napoleon I, bestowed upon Roger Ducos,
e of Napoleon's colleagues in the Provisional
nsulate, who had many of the buildings pulled down.
e château was later restored to the Orléans family
d is today the property of the Count of Paris;
merly one of the jewels of Touraine, it has been
ilt by unfortunate restorations and additions.

Conspirators' Balcony
and façade of the
Château of Amboise,
looking towards the Loire

The Salamander emblem of François I

Below the château stands the small manor of Le Clos ıcé where François I housed Leonardo da Vinci from 16 until his death on 2 May 1519. This charming ifice was built in 1477 by a major-domo of Louis XI; it François I spent much of his childhood with his other, Louise of Savoy; it contains a small collection models of machines invented by the brilliant Italian whose hand are – dubiously – attributed the traces of escoes seen in the chapel.

Opposite the château, on the other side of the Amasse, small centre of population existed as far back as the allo-Roman period; it later developed around the elfth-century Church of St Denis and the Church of Florentin, built on the orders of Louis XI. The bridges re cross the river by way of the Ile d'Or, or Ile Saint-ın, which was, according to tradition, the place where lovis met Alaric, the King of the Goths, in 496. estroyed for the first time by the Norsemen in 838, e bridges carried until the eighteenth century the ain road to Spain' by way of Chartres and Poitiers; in e sixteenth century this was known as the 'main road om Normandy, Maine, Perche and Anjou for travel-ıg to Touraine and Guyenne'. Amboise lost its ıportance as a crossroads when the big new road was ade through Tours and when the roads from Chartres d Le Mans were linked. The town of Amboise was mbarded in 1940 but, after rebuilding, it is now a pidly expanding industrial centre.

The high ground between the Loire and the Cher to e south of Amboise is covered by a large forest, at hose edge rises the curious pagoda of Chanteloup, flected in the water of its vast lake. This is all that remains of a magnificent château built during the Regency by Jean d'Aubigny. In 1761 the domain was bought by the Duke of Choiseul, who had been appointed Governor General of Touraine the previous year; he transformed the château into a large building with two storeys and attics, joined by colonnades to two wings. In this building Choiseul, exiled from the court for four years (1770–74) for having incurred the displeasure of the Countess du Barry, gave a series of sumptuous parties for all his visitors and guests, writers, artists and courtiers; the building was purchased, in 1832, by a real-estate broker, who completely demolished it. In memory of the steadfast support of his friends while he was in exile, Choiseul entrusted architect Le Camus with the construction of this elegant pagoda; built between 1775 and 1778 with seven storeys, it is entirely consecrated to the cult of the Chinese style which at that time was invading all forms of decoration.

On the other side of the Amboise forest, on the banks of the Cher or, more exactly, above that river, rises one of the most beautiful of Renaissance buildings. In the early years of the sixteenth century the Marques family, owners of the domain of Chenonceaux since 1243, were ruined. It was bought by Thomas Bohier, Comptroller-General of Finance in Normandy, who pulled down the old château and started a new one; the architect's name is unknown although Pierre Neveu, who worked at Chambord, has been suggested. The new château was completed in 1521, thanks to the efforts of Catherine Briçonnet while her husband Bohier was kept in Italy involved in the administration of the duchy of Milan.

The Chanteloup pagoda
near Amboise

The rectangular mass of the Château of Chenonceau is supported on two masonry piles set into the riv Cher; the staircase to the first storey is roofed by ogival vault supported by bare beams. The work Italian artisans is evident in the details of the decoratio After Gaillon, this is the first Renaissance château, bu somewhat prior to Azay-le-Rideau and Chambord.

For the settlement of his father's estate, Bohier's s found it necessary to cede the château to François Henry II then gave it to Diane de Poitiers in 1547. It w she who had the bridge built over the river as previous planned by Bohier, to the designs of Philibert Delorm On the death of the king, Catherine de Medici forc Diane to give up Chenonceaux in exchange for Cha mont and had a large, three-storeyed gallery built ov the bridge; the architect was probably Denis Courti Catherine gave magnificent entertainments at t château as well as 'triumphs', like the one in 156 stage-managed by Le Primatice. In the eighteen century, Madame Dupin, wife of a *fermier-génér* revived the tradition of brilliant receptions, which dre a mention from Jean-Jacques Rousseau.

Downstream from Amboise, as far as the junction the Vienne and the Loire, the hills flanking the increa ingly wider valley of the Loire are covered with vin whose cultivation, more than any other factor, h contributed to the prosperity of Touraine. Viticultu has been practised for a long time in this region, but t area under cultivation has decreased greatly since 188 becoming stabilized at some six thousand acres arou 1950. For the most part the individual vineyards a small because the cultivation of a vineyard as well as t

Château of Chenonceaux

aking and storing of the wine is a highly skilled ofession requiring scrupulous and constant attention; ere are about thirty thousand vine-growers in ouraine. Vine-growers' guilds with luscious names ve been formed in many wine-producing centres; ce in a while they hold 'chapter meetings in their wine llars, attended by their dignitaries, in order to extol, ith feastings worthy of Rabelais – whose memory is ways present – the merits of their wines and to wel- me new members into the guild after putting them rough rigorous initiation ordeals. The best-known hite wines are those from the Vouvray hills upstream om Tours; the principal red wines come from the hinon area on one hand and the region of Bourgueil on e other. Poets and writers have become lyrical about the cool-tasting white wines of the district, and the red wines with their *bouquet* of raspberry or violets; and all of them have exalted the digestive virtues of these wines.

In former days, the ease of communication provided by the Loire assisted this wine trade, and the produce of certain vineyards used to travel downstream to Nantes for shipment to the West Indies. An interesting wine museum has been installed in a lovely eighteenth-century dwelling at Rochecorbon, above which stands the 'Lantern', one of the corbelled turrets of a château which has disappeared; rock-cut cellars house wine-presses. At Tours itself, an ancient wine-press has been placed in the middle of the cloister of Saint-Julien, opposite the magnificent cellars of that twelfth-century abbey.

Vouvray: asparagus bed in the Loire valley

Tours with its industrial areas has become a larg
centre with more than 200,000 inhabitants; originall
however, it was concentrated on the banks of the Loir
While it is not known whether there was a primitiv
Gaulish settlement on the right bank, it is certain that th
Romans preferred to build their camp on the left ban
on a hill rising above flood level, where the cathedr
and the château were later built. 'Caesarodunum',
free city and the capital of the Turone tribe, enjoyed
period of peace and prosperity for nearly three hundre
years, during which temples to Roman deities we
built as well as an amphitheatre larger than the arena
Nîmes. In the fourth century this amphitheatre becam
a bastion in the rectangular enclosure built for protectio
against the approaching tide of Barbarian invasions.

Christianity got off to a slow start at Tours; in th
third century, the priests found the townsfolk so host
that they had to take refuge in grottoes on the rig
bank where, in later days, the powerful Abbey
Marmoutier was built. It was not until the end of th
sixth century that Gregory of Tours built the fi
church in the town; it survived into the twelfth centur
But in the Christian cemetery west of the town, outsi
the walls, chapels had already been built over the grav
of the saintly bishops of Tours; over that of St Marti
for instance, who died at Candes in 397, his body havi
been brought back to Tours, where increasing
numerous crowds of pilgrims came to pray, and a su
cession of ever more sumptuous edifices were erecte
Under the Carolingian kings, the religious commun
which grew up around St Martin's basilica becam
centre of learning and arts whose influence radiat

Wine harvest

rough the whole of France and parts of Europe; under e direction of the monk Alcuin, a protégé of Charle- agne, the 'scriptorium' became celebrated for the agnificent calligraphy of its manuscripts.

Raiding Norsemen, however, put an end to this osperity in the middle of the ninth century; in 853 the y, the basilica and its dependencies were set on fire; ither was Marmoutier spared; the relics of St Martin gan their peregrinations. Charles the Bald then built w fortifications around the city, but St Martin's silica remained unprotected and was surrounded by fensive walls only in 918. Known as Châteauneuf, the w city was almost entirely annihilated in 997 by a fire hich destroyed twenty-two churches. Treasurer Hervé Buzançais rebuilt the church on a much larger scale; was consecrated in 1014 and survived until the Revo- tion, having undergone many alterations. A single ceinte enclosing both Châteauneuf and city was built, it not until 1354. Reconstruction of the cathedral rted in the middle of the thirteenth century, and the ork went on slowly until the sixteenth; the edifice, erefore, bears witness to the evolution of technical ethods and of decoration during three centuries.

From the tenth to the thirteenth century, Blois was at e centre first of the feudal struggles between the counts Blois and the counts of Anjou for possession of ouraine, and then of the wars between the kings of ngland, who were also counts of Anjou and Touraine, d the kings of France. The capture of Chinon in 1205 it an end to English rule in Touraine, but it was not finitely attached to the Crown until the treaty of 28 ay 1258. In 1030 the capital of Touraine was con- nected with the right bank of the Loire by a bridge ending north of the cathedral; nearby, about 1160, King Henry II of England reconstructed a château built over the foundations of a Roman tower; only one tower of the enceinte survives. Charles VII liked to stay here, or in a rustic residence outside the walls known as 'Les Motils', where his son constructed a pleasant château. During the Hundred Years' War, neither the château nor the city of Tours was ever taken by the English. Joan of Arc came to Tours to equip herself with armour before going to Orléans. In the main east–west street of the town, formerly part of the road between Amboise and Chinon, one is still shown the 'Maison de la Pucelle Armée' where Joan's armourer, Colas de Montbazon, used to have a shop.

Like his father, Louis XI took pleasure in Tours and its surroundings; this attachment enriched the treasury of St Martin, and it was to that king that Tours owed both an improved city administration and the establishment of new industries, silk manufacture, for example. During the reign of Charles VIII the town was much improved; industries enjoying wide privileges evolved in response to new needs; increasing wealth allowed magnificent mansions to be constructed; the population increased. After the Italian expeditions, workmen from beyond the Alps brought new techniques and new tastes to Tours. Velvet began to be woven, and cloth of gold and of silver, satin and taffeta, all of which were not only despatched to distant places, but also sold locally in the tax-free fairs set up by François I. Sumptuous fêtes were held, and mystery plays were performed. All the arts developed under brilliant masters: sculpture with

Carved corbels on houses
in Plumereau Square, Tours

Following pages:
wine harvest at Vouvray

Michel Colombe, who was joined by Italian maste
such as the Justes; stained glass with Pinaigrier, paintin
with Fouchet and Bourdichon, not to mention gold
smiths, armourers, trough-makers, embroiderers an
others; the art of printing also developed: it was in fa
Touraine's great period.

The Wars of Religion dealt a terrible blow to all th
prosperity; but once peace had returned, industr
started up again, particularly the silk factories, as a resu
of the measures taken by Henry IV and, subsequentl
by Colbert whose brother became Inspector of Tourain
During the seventeenth century the town's populatio
increased considerably to the number of 80,000 sou
around the year 1670; in 1801 the figure was no mor
than 22,000. During the eighteenth century, in fact, in
dustry started to decline in the Touraine region, a
though this did not prevent big projects from bein
undertaken. About 1750 a plan was conceived for th
construction of a vast monumental complex (a bridg
over the Loire and the approaches to it) in imitation o
similar undertakings carried out in Paris. The first ston
of the bridge was laid in 1765, though the work was no
completed until 1779; the rue Transversaine – toda
called rue Nationale – begun in 1765, was more or le
completed just before the Revolution. The decline o
industry in Touraine continued throughout the whol
of the nineteenth as well as the early years of th
twentieth century.

The Second World War spared neither the town no
its industries; in June 1940, the German artiller
systematically destroyed an area in the town centre o
both sides of the rue Nationale; in addition, Tours wa

ombarded by the Allies thirty-seven times. After the
beration, local interests on their own initiative, while
ttending to the wounds inflicted by the war, instituted
series of measures designed to bring new life to local
ıdustries, at the same time laying down a bold policy
or housing and urban development. Eight industrial
ones have been created and equipped in an area close to
'ours and some of them have already been completely
lled. The municipality has also undertaken the massive
ısk of adjusting the course of the Cher; as a first step,
ıany fields below flood level have been filled in and are
ow built-up, inhabited areas; the second stage, of
raightening the river's course, will permit a large area
) be reclaimed, on which eighteen thousand dwellings
ould be built. These urban development projects will
e completed by an important programme of road con-
ruction related to the projected motorway from
ordeaux, which is now in process of being built. Is not
ours a 'crossroads town by right of geographical birth'
3runhes) standing between the two great international
ighways: from Switzerland to the Atlantic Ocean and
om the northern countries to Spain? Nor have the
orting and leisure requirements of a growing popula-
on been forgotten: stadia, a large swimming-pool and
ı immense lake for sailing have been created at the
ıtes of the town. The university and the cultural acti-
ties of the town are in full expansion. The old quarters,
ith their wealth of houses dating from the Middle
ges, the Renaissance and the neo-classical period, are
ther being completely restored or renovated in such a
ay that modernity and antiquity rub shoulders – all
is in order to attract tourists. The Loire itself is to

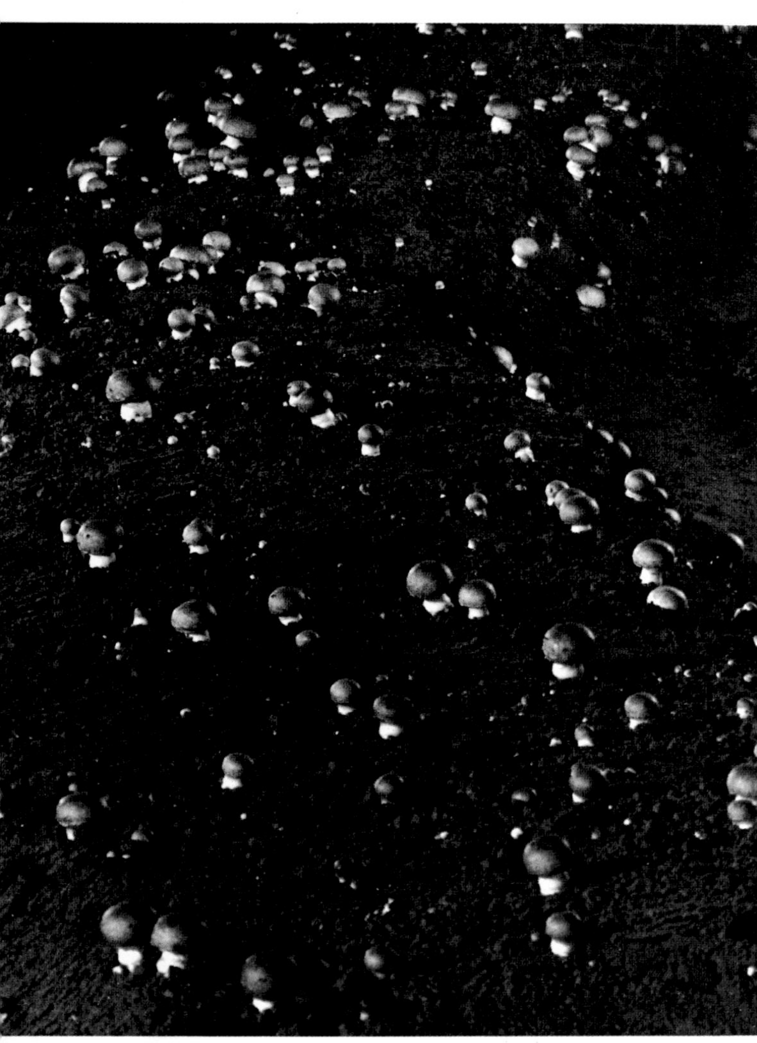

Stalactites and mushrooms
in the 'gutter caves',
Savonnières

experience a revival of activity – due to hovercraft whicl
will allow passengers to admire, from the middle of th
river, the châteaux and landscapes on both banks. Toda
Tours is a young town run by dynamic and confiden
men; one might say that Tours is the central metropoli
of France without being its capital.

The town of Tours is the centre of an urban area ex
tending along the right bank of the Loire as well as botl
banks of the Cher. The valleys of the two rivers in fac
unite into one single valley below the Montlouis ter
race, and the Cher continues to flow parallel to the Loir
for fifteen miles until their junction opposite Cinq-Mars
Between the two rivers, pasturelands and cornfield
stretch as far as the outskirts of Berthenay where, at th
edge of the town, two buildings steeped in history de
mand attention: the Priory of Saint-Cosme-en-l'Ile
rising at the edge of the Loire, and the manor o
Plessis-les-Tours.

The priory owes its name to a small chapel built in th
tenth century by Geldouin de Saumur on an islan
which, in the eighteenth century, became joined to th
left bank through the silting-up of a Loire arm. Thi
isolated place became a priory in 1092, four years afte
the death of Archdeacon Bérenger, who went there t
expiate his heresy. The buildings pertaining to a priory
church, refectory, cloister, etc., were built at the expens
of the collegiate Church of Saint-Martin. In the fifteent
century, considerable new work was undertaken, thank
to the liberality of Louis XI; in the sixteenth century
Pierre de Ronsard became prior *in commendam* in Marc
1565, and it was at the priory that he wrote many of h
works; he died there on 27 December 1585 and wa

Basket-maker's workshop
at Villaines

ried in the choir of the church. In 1742 the priory was olished and the buildings left to decay; during the evolution, the priory domain was split up. It was re-nstructed about 1926, thanks to the liberality of a rich tron, but Allied bombardments during the war caused me damage, although not to the tomb of Ronsard, hose remains had been rediscovered in 1933. Saint-osme belongs today to the Department (of the Indre d Loire); of the old priory there remain the twelfth-ntury monks' refectory, the apse with one of its apels, also twelfth century, and some elements from e fifteenth century, including the prior's residence here, according to tradition, Ronsard died on the first or.

The manor of Plessis-les-Tours was built by Louis XI tween 1463 and 1473 on the site of an older house; andoned by his successors, sold as a national asset and ree-quarters demolished and turned into a farm; fortu-tely it became the property of the town of Tours in 32. Today only the main living quarters exist; built of one and brick, they have undergone many alterations the course of the centuries. Two wings, no longer tant, used to complete the building; the principal urtyard was surrounded by an arcaded gallery and a aircase rose inside a small, octagonal tower. Despite all at has been written, this château was not a sombre rtress; breaking with the architectural traditions of e twelfth and thirteenth centuries, it is a distinct vance over all earlier constructions. Its simple façades ith their regular rows of mullioned windows and of rmer windows breaking the line of the sharply slop-g, slate-covered roofs, are in harmony with the surrounding scenery and the undulating line of the hills visible on the left bank of the Cher.

At Savonnières, at the foot of those hills, curious 'gutter caves' penetrate the rising ground not far from a church with a beautiful twelfth-century Romanesque doorway; from their roofs, shining with thousands of stalactites, drips water carrying calcareous salts which cover with a hard, white deposit whatever incongruous objects may be lying on the floor. In other caves, edible fungi grow abundantly on warm beds of compost. Two miles away rises the Château of Villandry, on the site of a manor which was called Colombiers until the sixteenth century. It was there, in 1189, that Philippe Auguste met Henry II, King of England, and the latter agreed to do homage to the King of France for his fiefs on the Continent. About 1532, François I's Secretary of State, Jean le Breton, had the present château built in the purest Renaissance style; one of his descendants succeeded in having the lordship raised to the rank of a marquisate, with the title of Villandry. In the eighteenth century another owner began to transform the building in the taste of the day but, fortunately, one of the most recent owners has restored it to its original state, and also reconstructed the gardens and terraces which were abandoned in the eighteenth century. The château consists of a principal courtyard, open to the north and looking over the valley, with the house built round the other three sides, along which runs a gallery carried on very ornate arches, and with high dormer windows in the attic roofs. The square keep of the old manor survives. On the front of the village church is a rare mounting block, which could also be used for preaching.

Luynes: the château

Close to Villandry and not far from the junction of the Cher and the Loire, a small arm of the Cher, following a course parallel to the Loire, joins up with the complex network of the arms of the Indre near Bréhémont. The latter river, having surrounded with its waters the Châteaux of Azay-le-Rideau and Islette, and passed within sight of the Château of Ussé, runs into the Loire above the atomic plant of Chinon. The waters of the Indre, formerly used for soaking hemp – an important Touraine industry – now serve to irrigate beds of osiers and reeds which are transformed into thousands of basket-work objects by the expert hands of the artisans of Villaines near the Chinon forest.

A few miles north of Villaines the elegant Châte of Azay-le-Rideau, in a setting of willows and horn beams, is reflected in the waters of the Indre. At the er of the fifteenth century, after experiencing the battles the Middle Ages as well as the vicissitudes of the Hundr Years' War, this château became the property of Mart Berthelot, who was private treasurer to King Louis and Charles VIII. His son was appointed Inspecto General of Finances for Normandy by Jacques Beaune-Semblançais and later became one of the fo treasurers of France. Married to Philippa Lesbah cousin of Catherine Briçonnais, mistress of Chenon ceaux, Berthelot decided to built a château on the site

Luynes: the Roman aquaduct

ı old manor-house. The château has the incomparable lvantage of having been built in one spurt of activity ıd of having come down to us without major modi- :ations. Begun in 1518, it was finished in 1528; as at henonceaux, the construction work was superintended / a woman, Philippa Lesbahy, but the name of the chitect is unknown. The château consists of two uildings placed at right angles to each other and built ı piles driven into the river Indre. The corner towers ıd the parapet walks are no doubt reminiscent of the chitecture of feudal times, then not long past, but the wers are softened by mouldings and the machicola- ons are purely decorative. The principal entrance, :low three storeys of windows flanked by small lumns and niches, gives access to a large wide stair- se with straight, parallel hand rails beneath a caisson ıult decorated with medallions. Gilles Berthelot fell to royal disfavour along with Beaune-Semblançais, ıd King François I confiscated the château. It passed rough the hands of various owners before being quired by the nation in 1905. It is now used as a enaissance museum and in summer it is the centre- ece of one of the most spectacular performances of *Son Lumière*.

Following the right bank of the Loire downstream om Tours as far as the Château of Rochecotte, where alleyrand used to visit his niece, the Duchess of Dino, e traveller can see that the river flows almost all the ay along the foot of the chalky slopes on which perch e Châteaux of Luynes, Cinq-Mars and Langeais. The hâteau of Luynes occupies a site which was known ıtil the seventeenth century by the name of Maillé; the

Interior of a tow
in the Château of Cinq-Ma

name was changed when the domain was acquired by Charles d'Albert, Lord of Luynes in Provence and a minister of Louis XIII, on his elevation to the rank of Duke of Luynes and Peer of France. The site was already inhabited in Gaulish times, and the Romans built an important edifice there, a fortified camp or a villa, to judge from the aqueduct of which forty piers are still standing, and a series of eight stone-and-brick arches still more or less intact. This aqueduct used to bring water from the source of the Pie Noire to a reservoir close to which the foundations of a Gallo-Roman villa with lovely mosaics have been discovered; it is a valuable relic of the great Gallo-Roman period in Touraine. At the beginning of the feudal period a fortified house belonging to the counts of Blois was built on the site; it was destroyed several times and was then rebuilt by the lords of Maillé and remained the property of their successors until the fifteenth century. The keep disappeared in 1658. The château forms a square, its walls flanked by round thirteenth-century towers in which wide windows were inserted in the fifteenth century. These towers and the curtain walls are rather badly matched. The entrance to the château between its two massive towers once had a drawbridge in front of it. On the west side, four towers with pepper-pot roofs overlook a small valley. On the south side, the architect Le Muet constructed a building around 1650 of which hardly any trace survives; in its place stands a terrace looking over the valley beyond the white houses crouching at the foot of the château. Inside the square, an elegant fifteenth-century stone-and-brick pavilion backs on to the west curtain wall; it has an octagonal staircase tower dating from 1465.

At Cinq-Mars, as at Luynes, one monument surviv
which recalls the great Roman period of Touraine. It is
huge square pile – or pillar – over which rise four small
pillars. Bricks carefully placed round this mass of ston
work form a decorative pattern, but no historical da
exist to indicate the date and purpose of this monumen
Cinq-Mars, like Luynes, was the name of one of Lou
XIII's favourites. The domain of Cinq-Mars was only
barony until 1630 when it was raised to the dignity of
marquisate for the benefit of Henri de Ruzé, son
Marshal Effiat; he became a member of the royal cour
thanks to Richelieu's protection, and was used by th
latter to oppose Mademoiselle de Hautfort's influen
over the king. In 1639 he obtained the post of Intenden
General of the Royal Stables, but was beheaded at Lyo
in 1642 after being convicted of treason.

Shortly after this event, the old château of the lords
Cinq-Mars, dating from the eleventh century, was di
mantled; all that remains of this imposing building, th
site of which is still surrounded by particularly de
moats and various outlying defensive works, are tw
enormous, round, thirteenth-century towers enclosir
large ogival-vaulted rooms the walls of which we
pierced in the fifteenth century to make openings f
wide windows. These ruins are in a restful setting. Th
terrace looks over the Loire flowing quietly in its sand
bed through fields divided by rows of poplars. Belo
the towers stretches the long street of rock-hewn dwel
ings, with flowers hanging on their high walls. Th
small town of Cinq-Mars, encircling its old tent
century church, has often been mentioned as an examp
of a typical Touraine village.

Below Cinq-Mars the Loire, having received the waters of the Cher a little way upstream, runs in a wider valley, which becomes broader and brighter upon reaching Langeais. André Theuriet wrote a poem at this very spot:

> 'Wide and slow in the midday sun
> The Loire glides gleaming through the fields;
> Girt with poplars, alders, birch trees
> Green islands doze on the shining stream;
> From the vines to the ripening corn all is love,
> A muted murmur, a sensual song;
> In wordless rapture the Loire
> Enfolds the gnarled willows in passionate embrace.'

What a contrast between the luminous valley and the enormous black mass of the Château of Langeais, rising not on a height, but in the midst of the white houses of the town! Behind it, beyond the flowers in the lovely gardens, the ruins of the first château stand at the eastern end of the rocky promontory around the north of which flows a small river, the Roumer.

Of this early château, which seems to have survived until the fifteenth century, only the eastern and northern walls of the keep remain; in 1428 when the English, who had been in occupation, surrendered the place to the French in exchange for a sum of money, a clause in the articles of surrender stipulated that 'the château shall be knocked down and razed to the ground, except the big tower'; the western and southern walls, however, were not demolished until 1841.

This keep is an extremely important monument both historically and from the point of view of military archaeology, for it is thought to be the oldest of a surviving keeps and, therefore, the prototype of th keeps of Montbazon, Loches and Lavardin. Accordin to the chronicles, it was built about 994 by the Count c Anjou, Foulques Nerra, then in process of warrin against the counts of Blois, but the possibility cannot b ruled out that fortifications of some sort existed on th spot at an earlier date. The promontory, on which th keep stands, is narrow and easily defensible; the we side is protected by a deep ditch beyond which trac have been found of a motte, an earthen mound whic could have supported forward defences or a woode keep. Like the other keeps built by Foulques Nerra Touraine, for example that at Montbazon, the keep Langeais formed an elongated rectangle with thic walls. It originally consisted of a ground floor with tw unvaulted floors above it. As in all keeps of the tim there were no openings at ground-floor level; the floo above do not seem to have had fireplaces. The walls a of cemented rubble between two layers of sma rectangular dressed stones and show signs of freque repair. Stone and brick alternate in the archstones of th openings. In 1428, after the English had left, Langea again became a Crown property, and Charles VII a pointed governors for the place and it was there that 1460 the Charter of Touraine was first written down

After Charles VII's death in 1461, it seems that Lou XI very quickly made up his mind to start building th present château, since Jean Briçonnet, Mayor of Tou and Intendent-General of Finance, was made responsib for 'paying for the work and the buildings of th Château of Langeais in 1465 and 1467'. The work w

Remains of the donjon of Foulques Nerra at Langeais

tainly completed about 1490, because on 8 December
91 the wedding of Charles VIII and Anne of Brittany
ok place 'in the said château of Langès', in the presence
the future Louis XII and the Chancellor of France,
y de Rochefort. Langeais remained Crown property
til 1631 when, after rather tortuous proceedings, it
s granted to Louise of Lorraine, widow of the Prince
Conti, in exchange for Chinon, which was coveted
Richelieu. Then, after becoming the property of
rious owners by purchase or inheritance, it was sold in
97 and its nineteenth-century owners, instead of
molishing it, repaired it and kept it in good condition.
day it is owned by the Institut de France, to whom it
was left in 1904 under the terms of the will of Jacques Siegfried, together with all the works of art he had collected over ten years.

The château stands a short distance below Foulques Nerra's keep. It is essentially a military edifice, with an unpleasing and menacing exterior, designed for defence and protection of the royal residences at Tours, du Plessis and Amboise in the troubled times of the League for the Public Good. The entrance, with its modern drawbridge and two flanking towers, resembles the door of a prison; the larger of these towers, known as the keep, together with the entrance building, forms a defensive system in itself, independent of the two wings

Château of Ussé:
towers and dormer windows

Silk hangings in one of the bedrooms ▶

Following pages:
Château of Azay-le-Rideau
reflected in its moat

stretching to the southeast. The exterior walls of the building formerly plunged down into moats filled with water from the Roumer river; they are well built and contain narrow, mullioned windows. A parapet walk runs round the whole building, including the three eastern towers with their pepper-pot roofs; it is crenellated, full of loopholes and machicolations. From the courtyard inside the walls one gains a less austere impression and one can sense the dawning of that taste for air and light which reached its apogee in the châteaux conceived and constructed by and for women, such as Azay-le-Rideau and Chenonceaux. At Langeais the windows opening on the courtyard are wider and high dormer windows break the blue row of the steep, slate-covered attic roofs, which have preserved their fifteenth-century timbers. The main body of the building, designed as the living quarters, is flanked by two staircase towers with bevelled corners, the rooms are all intercommunicating and the original fireplaces, stone seats and most of the ceilings still survive. The south wing was reserved for entertainments and has large reception rooms, such as the one where the wedding of Anne of Brittany and Charles VIII took place.

Downstream from Langeais, on the right bank of the Loire, where the line of chalky cliffs continues, one is still in Touraine as far as Ingrandes, where the Bourgueil plain begins; it was once part of Anjou. On the left bank, the Touraine lands stretch even further, a lan scape offering a differing aspect, as far as the junction the Viette and the Loire. At first, from Bréhémont a as far as Néman where the Indre flows into the Loire, t many arms of this tributary are overshadowed by t dark foliage of the Chinon forest, out of which rises t Château of Ussé, with its terraces descending towar the Indre.

Man has lived in this region from remote antiquity. the beginning of feudal times there certainly existed stronghold with a keep, part of which was included the ground floor of the now existing keep. The main pa of the château, however, dates from the fifteenth ce tury, when the domain of Ussé became the property the Beuil family in 1462; the Beuils were followed three generations of Espinays between 1485 and 155 After 1557, the ownership of the property changed co tinually until 1659, when the château was bought Louis Bernin de Valentinay, Comptroller-General the Royal Household, whose son married Vauba daughter in 1691. Important alterations carried out du ing the sixteenth and seventeenth centuries have be wrongly attributed to Vauban. Like Langeais, t château escaped destruction at the time of the Revol tion, and it is still inhabited.

Having originally formed a square, the building n consists of three wings; the northern wing was dem

The nuclear station of Chin
at Néman: from left to rig
Unit I, Unit II, Unit

The pleasures of fishing
the Loire at Chou

lished by a member of the Espinay family so as to open the courtyard to light and air, as was done at Chaumont. The southern and eastern wings, as well as what remains of the northern wing, are entirely Gothic; the western wing, despite various alterations, preserves a number of Renaissance features. The keep, the oldest part of the château, and a small seventeenth-century house, adjoin this western wing. The eastern wing used to contain the main doorway between two towers, but the door has been replaced by a window. Beside it stood the old chapel, with its east end projecting above the curtain wall. A charming, small, octagonal lantern is corbelled out from the front of this wing. The southern wing has preserved its original aspect, with Gothic decorations on the gables of its dormer windows.

In many features the château resembles Langeais and also Le Plessis-Bourrée in Anjou; the towers with their crenellated, loopholed parapet walks built out on moulded corbels are similar; the curtain walls are also topped by such parapet walks. It is consequently possible to date the Gothic parts of the Château of Ussé to the period between 1462 and 1490. This château is, however, much less austere than Langeais and it is certainly much less sombre in colour, thanks to the slightly ochre-tinted tufa, which explodes into light when floodlit for *Son et Lumière*. It is more a country house than a château, of the type sometimes known as a 'Sleeping Beauty' château. Inside, the walls of the rooms, especially the King's Room, are hung with old silks. Below, the courtyard terraces, which were already completed in 1699, are today gay with flowerbeds and centuries-old orange trees.

A little way from the château, Charles d'Espin
built between 1523 and 1535 a wonderful chapel, whic
was consecrated in 1538. Entirely Gothic in conceptic
and design, this building is finely decorated inside
Italian Renaissance style. The chapel consists of a sing
nave of three bays, roofed with ogival vaults, havir
both liernes and tiercerons; the pentagonal choir h
pendent keystones. At the front, a very decorativ
triumphal arch stands over a porch with medallio
studded walls, out of which project the three-dime
sional busts of Christ and the Twelve Apostles; gracef
arabesques and foliated mouldings cover the pilaste
and the arch, surrounding a vast scallop. Inside, t
sixteenth-century carved choir stalls have been restore
to their original place. Together with the chapel
Champigny-sur-Veude and the collegiate Church
Montrésor, this chapel is one of the most successf
religious buildings of the sixteenth century.

Leaving Ussé and following the valley of the Indr
one arrives shortly before its junction with the Loire
the Chinon complex of nuclear power stations, the fir
to be built in France. They look somewhat odd in th
middle of the peaceful Loire landscape. The site w
chosen for the cooling facilities offered by the Loir
waters and the presence of a subsoil able to support th
exceptionally heavy weight of the steel and cement re
quired for the reactors. Nevertheless, it was necessary t
build many embankments to protect the power statio
from any floods and to construct a wide canal parallel t
the river to distribute the water. Each of the three powe
stations is an independent unit. Unit I, with its enormou
sphere and cooling tower, produced, on 26 Septemb

Château of Chinon

1956, the first electricity from nuclear power in France. Units II and III, together with their appurtenances, are large, almost cubic masses of masonry. The station staff live in residential areas built specially for them in the communes of Avoine and Bourgueil, on both sides of the river. The establishment of these nuclear centres at first disturbed the local inhabitants, upsetting their peaceful daily lives, but it has not kept them from following one of their favourite occupations, namely fishing in the Loire, where a variety of fish are to be found in abundance; seated in their flat-bottomed boats, they patiently wait for carp, pike and other fish to take the hook. Fewer and fewer people now stretch big nets across the Loire to fish for shad and salmon, but in the dead arms of the river eels are plentiful.

On the right bank opposite the power stations, the valley of Anjou opens out, extending back for several miles to the ill-defined hills of Restingé, Bourgueil and Saint-Nicolas, all covered with famous vineyards. The town of Bourgueil, on its gravel terrace, grew up around an abbey founded in 990 by a daughter of Thibaud le Tricheur, Count of Anjou; some eighteenth-century buildings survive. The plain of Bourgueil, a part of Anjou, was included in 1790 in the Department of Indre-et-Loire; it consists mainly of pastureland, but in the district of the Varennes-de-Loire early vegetables and fruit are grown in abundance, replacing the cultivation of rare plants introduced from Italy in earlier times, such as liquorice, aniseed and coriander; in the middle of the Varennes stands the charming stone-and-brick manor of the Réaux family made famous by the writings of Tallemant des Réaux. These fat lands of La

Chapelle and Chouzé are well protected against floods by Henry II Plantagenet's old levee.

On the left bank, between the Loire and the Vienne, the flint-bearing clays of the plateau on which the forest of Chinon stands run down into a peninsula formed of rich alluvial soil, the 'flat country of Verron', which begins at the gates of Chinon. This town is of very ancient origin; Rabelais attributes its foundation to Cain, 'the first town builder'. Chinon may justifiably call itself a 'royal town' since it has twice been the seat of the government of a kingdom, first under Henry II Plantagenet, King of England, and later during the reign of Charles VII. Throughout the centuries Chinon has been the scene of historic events. The impressive remains of its château overlooking the town recall, among other memories, the imprisonment of the Templar dignitaries (including Jacques Molay) and, above all, the time spent there by Joan of Arc after her interview with the king before she set out for Orléans. The old streets of the town with their wooden houses and sixteenth- and seventeenth-century mansions have since 1969 been in the process of complete renovation, particularly in the town centre at the 'Grand Carroi'; the funeral procession of Henry II and also no doubt that of Richard Cœur de Lion passed through here, and it also provided lodging for Joan of Arc while she waited for her audience with the king; it served too, as a meeting-place for the Estates General during the reign of Charles VII.

Chinon has a natural vocation as a tourist centre, with its great sweep of river, a camping ground affording unforgettable views of the château and the quays of the town, as well as excursion on the Loire and the Vienne The extremely fertile region of Le Verron with it strung-out villages produces early vegetables, potatoe and asparagus in particular, and also wine from th Breton wine stock of which Rabelais says, 'it grows no in Brittany, but in the good country of Verron'. At th extremity of the peninsula, the Vienne flows into th Loire running in its majestically wide bed, past Mont soreau, a village whose main street is an uninterrupte continuation of the main street of Candes, thoug Candes lies in Touraine and Montsoreau in Anjou. A old saying has it that 'neither sheep nor calves graze be tween Candes and Montsoreau'. It was at Candes tha St Martin, Bishop of Tours, died in 297. His disciple from Ligugé in Poitou kept vigil over his body with th intention of burying it at their monastery; but whil they were asleep – a condition allegedly assisted by number of libations – the faithful people of Tourain carried the body away, put it on a boat and rowed i triumphantly to Tours. On the site previously occupie by a small chapel, the construction of a large church wa begun in the twelfth century, of which the thirteenth century nave is one of the loveliest examples of Gothi architecture in Anjou. The nave and its equally hig aisles are roofed with sail-vaults, the ribs running dow to end on bases, carved with long human figures, at th top of very slender piers. The north porch is parti cularly remarkable for its decorative carvings and vau with ribs supported in the centre by a slender, mono lithic column. During the fifteenth century, the outsid of the building was given a military aspect by th addition of parapets, crenellations and machicolations

Château of Montsoreau
from the headland at Verron

In the middle of the village of Montsoreau, stretching long the Loire, rises the silhouette of the powerful hâteau which Alexander Dumas made famous with his ıle *The Lady of Montsoreau*, although the story as he ·lls it is rather far removed from historical fact. Before ıe opening of the present road, the north face of this uilding plunged straight down to the river; it was built y Jean de Chambes, husband of the heiress of Thibault 'II, Lord of Montsoreau and a member of King Charles VII's Privy Council, who held a number of iplomatic posts, in Venice in particular. Montsoreau ands at a point on the Loire which has always been a lace of strategic importance. A château built in the velfth century controlled both the road from Chinon) Saumur and the river traffic going up the Loire to 'ours and Orléans, as well as that on the Vienne going to Chinon; the tolls exacted until 1631 were a source of onsiderable income.

The present château must have been built about 1455 or it is known that in that year materials needed for the oofing reached the place under royal franchise; certain nbellishments were added in the course of the six-·enth century. The square, traditional fifteenth-century uilding with two solid, square, slightly projecting orner towers, surrounded by a deep moat filled with oire water, gives the impression of a stronghold with s parapet walks, machicolations and crenellations. It is uilt over vaulted cellars with floors above the highest ood level and the first storey is level with the interior ourtyard. Despite the presence, in certain rooms, of atures designed for defensive purposes, the place is not ·ally a medieval fortress. The façades contain wide, mullioned windows and the high attic has a double row of superimposed windows, the lower row being at the level of the parapet walk, while the dormer windows above them project as far as the vertical line of the façade to give light to the attics. The only decorative feature is the parapet walk with its moulded corbels.

When the château was built there was only one spiral staircase in a turret with a pepper-pot roof in the southwest corner of the courtyard to provide access to the different floors, where the big rooms with their double fireplaces were all intercommunicating. It was only about the year 1520 that another spiral staircase was built in the southeast corner; this one is of quite different character, being much wider and having four double windows opening to the light in the centre of the turret, which is roofed with a Flamboyant Gothic vault. The pilasters flanking these windows have delicate carvings, and the bas-reliefs between the windows portray fantastic scenes such as: two monkeys using pulleys to lift a block of stone with the device 'Je le Feray' ('I shall do it'), or a stag hiding behind a bush. The enceinte of the château enclosed a small chapel dedicated to St Michel, and formerly served by canons.

The Château of Montsoreau was left deserted for a long time and then sold in 1804 to various private persons, but it was fortunately bought up by the Department of Maine-et-Loire in 1912 and has been completely restored since then.

A road running through the township of Montsoreau, with its flower-decked fifteenth- and sixteenth-century houses hugging the slope of the hill, takes the traveller along a cool valley to the celebrated Abbey of Fontevrault. This was one of the richest and most importan abbeys ever to have existed in France, and the only on wherein a community of women and a community o men were subject to one and the same rule under th authority of an abbess. The founder of the abbey wa Robert d'Arbrissel, a fiery Breton preacher, who wishe to provide a permanent settlement in a solitary place fo the crowds of disciples – legend has it that there wer several thousand of them – who had been following hi through Anjou and the neighbouring provinces. H decided that the Vale of Fontevrault, where, as its nam indicates, there was a spring of water, was suitab for his purpose; gifts of land and quarries flowed i Robert d'Arbrissel has sometimes been considered th first feminist because he entrusted to a woman th government of his foundation, the statutes of whic were approved by Pope Paschal II in 1106 and confirme by Pope Calixtus II in 1119, at the time of consecratio of those parts of the church completed by that date; th statutes remained in force until the Revolutio Hersende de Champagne, the first prioress, was su ceeded by Abbess Petronille de Chemillé, who assume responsibility for the work of construction after Robe d'Arbrissel's death in 1117.

The abbey received important donations, notabl from the Plantagenets, some of whom were buri there. In the course of the centuries the influence of t abbey extended far and wide, not only in the dominio of the Plantagenets, but also in the centre of France a even into Spain. It had as dependencies more than o hundred priories and other important foundations a properties.

Abbey of Fontevrault:
profile of Henry II Plantagenet
on his tombstone

The thirty-six abbesses who succeeded each other were nearly all members of the high nobility or even of royal blood, such as Anne of Orléans, niece of Louis XII, Renée of Bourbon, whose energetic intervention put a stop to the decadence of the community which had set in during the fifteenth century, her niece Louise of Bourbon, and Jeanne-Baptiste of Bourbon, the legitimized daughter of Henri IV. Then came the sister of the Marchioness of Montespan, Madeleine de Rochechouart-Mortemart, nicknamed 'Queen of Abbesses'.

The community, which still consisted of more than a hundred nuns at the Revolution, was dispersed in 1790. The monastery, pillaged by the Huguenots in 1562, was sacked again and the works of art, the library and furniture all disappeared. In 1804 the place became a prison by virtue of a Napoleonic decree; the prison administration occupied the whole of the buildings and made some disastrous alterations. In 1904, however, the Direction-Générale des Beaux-Arts began to undertake a partial restoration but it was not until July 1963 that the penitentiary was abolished and evacuation of the place begun. Today, this unique group of buildings is well on the way to total restoration.

In its early years this was a veritable monastery town and it then comprised the Grand Moutier or principal monastery with its abbey church, cloister, convent buildings and a chapel dedicated to St Benedict, around which the abbesses in the sixteenth century had a variety of buildings erected: the Magdalene Convent for penitent young women, with its chapel and annexes, the Saint Lazarus Convent for the sick and the lepers, with its chapel and annexes and, at some distance to the north, the monastery for men, of which, unfortunately nothing remains.

The jewel of Fontevrault, the abbey church, is o surprisingly large dimensions. It was built in two period of building activity, first the choir and transept, an then the nave. The choir is separated by tall cylindrica columns from the wide ambulatory with its thre radiating chapels, and is roofed by a barrel-vault and half-dome; the transept, also, has a barrel-vault with small dome in the middle. There are hardly any decorative elements in these areas, whereas the nave, on th contrary, is particularly richly adorned, with very elaborate capitals. It has four domes on pendentives, a typ of construction widespread in Anjou, deriving fron relations between Fontevrault and the bishopric o Angoulême. The tombstones of Henry II of Englanc Eleanor of Aquitaine and Richard Cœur de Lion, as we as a wooden statue of Isabel, wife of John Lackland wer placed at the top of this nave; all these statues have bee moved around many times.

The original cloister and chapter-house to the sout of the church were reconstructed bit by bit during th sixteenth century, thus allowing us to follow the evolution of the different styles of decoration. The refector also, placed close to the south side of the cloister, w altered in the sixteenth century and covered with a ogival vault. It is an immense hall, and originally had timber roof. A curious building at the end of the refectory, called the Evrault Tower, used to house th abbey kitchens; it has for a long time excited the imag nation and ingenuity of historians and archaeologist some of whom see in it a baptistry, others a funerar

bey of Fontevrault:
mneys on the old kitchens

Following pages:
Château of Saumur

apel; although it has been damaged many times, the toration work carried out in 1902 has returned to it ore or less its original appearance. The ground plan is tagonal, with a small apse on each of the eight sides; e next floor is square, but over it the octagonal plan urns for the base of the central chimney or pyramid; h small apse has a separate fireplace and chimney. All se chimneys, shooting out of a roof covered with imcated stones, produce a most unusual effect. This is a pe of construction of which very few examples nain.

The Saint Lazarus Convent, the chapel with its aight east end, the Romanesque refectory and, between the two, a reconstructed sixteenth-century cloister, all join together to form a charming group of buildings. The Magdalene convent and the men's monastery disappeared as a result of alterations made while the place was being used as a prison. Abbess Renée of Bourbon, to whom we owe the first of the sixteenth-century reconstructions, had a tribune built against the wall of the transept arm, supported on an elegant arcade. The cloister, or court of St Benedict, built around the small twelfth-century chapel, is probably the work of Abbess Louise of Bourbon; its principal feature is a remarkable, rectilinear staircase with two landings.

After Montsoreau, the left bank of the Loire continues to run along at the foot of tufa hills hollowed out into grottoes, cave-dwellings and cellars; the villages as far as Saumur still contain many Renaissance houses.

The origin of the town of Saumur is rather obscure. It seems that Norsemen destroyed a monastery downstream from Angers, where the relics of Florent, who arrived in the fourth century to convert the people of Saumur, were preserved; Charles the Bald donated the monks a 'villa' at Saumur. No doubt walls were built to protect the place, but it was nevertheless devastated in 853 and the relics continued their peregrinations. In the tenth century, thanks to the generosity of a Count of Blois in whose domains Saumur was situated, a monastery was built to shelter the relics brought there by the monk Absalom. But in 1016 Foulques Nerra, Count of Anjou, seized Saumur, then held by Geldouin, a vassal of Eudes of Blois. A new disaster befell Saumur; Guy Geoffroy, Count of Poitiers, set fire to the château, the Church of Saint-Florent and several other churches.

It is certain that there existed a château at Saumur which was a key position in the wars between the kings of England and the kings of France. Philippe Auguste took possession of it in 1203, entrusted it to his steward, Guillaume de Roches, in 1206 and took it back again, finally, in 1207. It remained part of the royal domains until 1246 and during that time, probably around 1227–30, a new building was erected which became the foundation of the present château. The main parts of the latter date from the fourteenth century, as appears from details of accounts. In the fifteenth century it must have looked rather like the miniature contained in the calendar for the month of November of the *Très Ric* *Heures du Duc de Berry*. The grandson of Louis René of Anjou, had some work done on the château the fifteenth century; at his death in 1480, Saumur r turned to the Crown. Many of the inhabitants of Saum became Protestants at the Reformation, and Dupless Mornay, the 'Huguenot Pope' appointed Milita Governor-General by Henry of Navarre in 1589, car to live at the château. He strengthened the defences co siderably and made interior alterations which allow him to house his collections of tapestries, pictures a books of hours. In 1599, he created at Saumur t famous Protestant Academy to which students from parts of Europe came to study; Saumur became t metropolis of Protestantism.

Duplessis-Mornay left Saumur in 1621 and h departure marks the start of the château's decay. In 162 the town's fortifications were dismantled, with the e ception of those of the château. The Revocation of t Edict of Nantes in 1685 put an end to the town's pro perity and a great part of the population left. Duri the eighteenth century parts of the château collapsed

The arrival, in 1768, of a carabineer corps, for which magnificent barracks was built and a riding scho founded, brought back a little prosperity to the tow This school became the ancestor of the present caval school; it was abolished in 1791 and re-established 1814. In 1810 the château became a State prison. It w not until 1906 that the town of Saumur was able to b it from the State and start restoring it.

The town of Saumur was much damaged during t Second World War, being hit by more than a thousa

Gatehouse,
Château of Saumur

shells in the fighting of 19–22 June 1940; many buildings, including the château, were hit, in particular the areas in the vicinity of the bridges.

The château stands at the end of a promontory commanding the junction of the Loire and the Thouet. It is roughly square in shape, the four corner towers having round bases but becoming polygonal higher up; today there are only three wings along the sides of the interior courtyard. In the middle of the latter a large circular opening ventilates a big, almost-square underground chamber; nearby, a deep well provided the château's water supply. The different openings, both on the outside as well as those facing the courtyard, have been subjected to so many alterations that it has become impossible to tell what they were like originally.

The courtyard façade of the north wing is flanked by two staircase turrets, one of which has windows between hooded niches; a projecting structure has been built against this façade, supported on a series of wide arches carrying two superimposed corridors, which provide outside communication between the rooms of the principal municipal museum and the equestrian museum. The latter houses a wonderful collection of all appurtenances connected with horses, going back to prehistoric times, such as bits, stirrups, spurs from every country and period.

Nowadays the main entrance to the château leads over a wide ramp to the south side and ends at a miniature château with two corner turrets. The original entrance must have been on the east side under a projecting construction built against that wing, but it is no longer in use. The towers with their pepper-pot roofs are surrounded by machicolations which continue along th tops of some of the curtain walls. But alas! the spire chimneys, bell-turrets and weathercocks appearing the *Très Riches Heures* have disappeared.

The town of Saumur grew up first around the hill c which the château stands and the south end of the Loi bridge, which for centuries was the only one betwee Tours and Ponts-de-Cé; later, the town spread to th islands in the river and to the right bank. Many fifteenth and sixteenth-century buildings have survived i Saumur, for instance the charming edifice now servin as town hall, with its elegant latticed windows. On th small island of Offard stands the Manoir de l'Ile d'C associated with King René and his family; now know as the 'Queen of Sicily's House', this manor was bui long ago by Yolande of Aragon, wife of Louis II c Anjou, King of the Two Sicilies, and mother of Kin René; her daughter Marie married King Charles VI whom Queen Yolande did her best to influence i favour of Joan of Arc's enterprise.

Notre-Dame-de-Nantilly, the oldest church i Saumur, was built on the site of an old 'villa' mentione in a document dating from 848 and was at first the se of the Priory of Saint Florent. The present church, stand ing south of the château, dates from the twelfth century the nave is remarkable for the width of its barre vault, with thick transverse arches; the side walls a strengthened by a series of arches. The ten capitals in th nave make a uniform group and are among the mo outstanding pieces of Romanesque sculpture in Anjo palmettes on little stalks, monsters, lions, griffons wi intertwined tails, human faces with cats' ears and litu

Château of Saumur:
loggias in the inner courtyard

ical scenes, all prepare the spectator for the sculptures
Cunault and the bishops' palace at Angers. This church
so possesses an invaluable collection of seventeen
pestries from the fifteenth, sixteenth and seventeenth
nturies, among which special mention must be made
f the one portraying the *Dance of the Savages* (made
ound 1500). Two other sets of tapestries (the story of
Florent and the life of St Peter) are kept in another of
e town's churches, standing near the bridge, namely
int Peter in the Marsh. Burnt down in 1067 by the
ount of Poitiers, the choir and transept were rebuilt at
e end of the twelfth century, and the nave at the start
the thirteenth; the latter is roofed with eight-ribbed
mical vaults. This type of structure is purely Angevin,
it the influence of Aquitaine can still be felt.
Later, upstream at the edge of the Loire, a pilgrimage
olved in the fifteenth century around a supposedly
iraculous spring and the place where a *Pietà* was found
1454 buried in a clayey field (*ardilliers*), which gave its
me to the Church of Notre-Dame-des-Ardilliers. The
teenth-century nave, to which two chapels were
ded in the seventeenth century – one of them built by
ichelieu in fulfilment of a vow, was joined to a rotunda
by eight large windows and crowned with a cupola in
e style of the Italian Renaissance; the cupola was only
mpleted in 1695 by Madame de Montespan, who
ed to stay at Saumur with the General of the Order of
eachers, when visiting her sister, the Abbess of Fonte-
ault. The Church of Notre-Dame-des-Ardilliers,
cked by the Huguenots in 1562, was very badly
maged in 1944; today, the beauty of this quarter of
umur is enhanced by the presence of this tastefully

Basket-work horse's head and display of horseshoes in the Château of Saumur

restored church alongside the buildings of the Order o Preachers, wholly constructed of white tufa, with th row of their high slate roofs broken by stone-frame dormer windows.

Not far from Saumur, on the left bank of the Thoue are the ruins of one of the greatest of the Loire valle abbeys, the Abbey of Saint-Florent, 'the loveliest, in a Anjou'. After destruction in 1026 – when Saumur w taken by Foulques Nerra – of their monastery of Sain Florent-le-Vieil, which the monks had just built close the château, and after an unsuccessful attempt by Cou Foulques to persuade them to move to Angers with th relics of the saint, they settled on the banks of th Thouet. This great abbey church was demolished 1805 and all that remains of it is the porch and a cryp The porch, built in 1203, today serving as the chapel a convent, is roofed with a remarkable vault in th Angevin style; square at the base, it becomes an octago over half-domed squinches. The crypt, rectangular wi a semicircular east end, was built between 1028 ar 1030; it consists of three bays under groined vaults, su ported on monolithic columns with simply carv capitals. In the parish of Saint-Hilaire-Saint-Floren squeezed between the Thouet and the slopes where th bubbling wine of Saumur is made, there are yet tw other churches which were dependencies of the abbe

South of Saumur, on the other side of the Thou stands the biggest dolmen in Anjou, in the middle of th village of Bagneux, forming a covered alley; it consis of twenty-one pieces of sandstone, sixteen of the placed vertically in the ground and four serving as roo ing; the last one is lying on the ground. Close by,

Field of leek seeds in the Loire valley near Gennes

Interior of the Bagne
dolmen near Saum

Following pag
the Loire in flo

menhir, still erect, called the 'Little Roofed Stone', stands together with another, smaller dolmen almost in line with the big one, known as the 'Long Stone'.

This entire region is one of the earliest inhabited areas of France. There are many traces of the prehistoric people who lived in the Saumurois and Anjou; in the Loire valley itself one can visit the prehistoric hearths of Saint-Lambert-des-Levées, the Magdalene dolmen near Gennes, those at Bazouillère close to the Thouriel, the Bretellière menhir in the Mauges area and the Fairy House at Saint-Lambert-les-Poteries. This series of megalithic monuments is a prolongation of the prehistoric sites in Touraine and the valley of the Vienne below Grand-Pressigny, where the dolmens of Crouzilles, Briançon and Thizay are, not to mention the megaliths on both sides of the valley of the Loire, such as the Pontigné dolmen near Baugé and the covered alley of Pierre-Folle, close to Bournant. Prehistoric fortified sites and enclosures used to stand on the hills overlooking the valley; they may have been occupied later by Roman troops, which is why they are now known as 'Roman camps' – for example the circle of Cinais in the valley of the Vienne. Not far downstream from Saumur, near to the place where the Rû d'Enfer enters the Loire, the camp of Chênehutte-les-Tuffeaux was doubtless a Roman town; despite much damage, its stone-and-earth walls have come down to us.

From the top of the hills on the left bank of the Loire, whether at Candes or Saumur or Chênehutte, one of the most beautiful landscapes of the whole valley extends. Between the Varennes of Bourgueil and the river bed, broad alluvial deposits stretch between Bourgueil and Ponts-de-Cé. The Authion and its tributary, the Lath with its many arms run for miles parallel to the course the Loire, as did the Cisse, the Cher and the Indre. Tl whole region, known as 'La Vallée', was former covered with an immense forest, but its aspect chang when clearings were made in the early Middle Ages. large part of La Vallée remained subject to flooding a consequently this region was the birthplace of the fi dikes, the proper word for which is *turcies* in t Angevin dialect. To start with, levees made of earth a turf with stakes and fascines provided a permanent ro along the river and served to protect the most expos areas, but this was not enough. It is evident from ordinance dated 821 that Louis the Pious was thinki of building dikes; but it was Henry II Plantagenet, 1160, who, in the fields of Saint-Florent in the presen of the principal lords of the Bourgueil and Saum region, promulgated his famous charter dealing with t *turcies* of the Loire. In an attempt to ensure the prop maintenance of the dikes, Henry II sought to establi settlements of 'guests' exempt from all feudal servic but whose job at all times was to see to the building a maintenance of such works. The cover of this protecti produced an influx of people into the rich lands of t valley. The levees in Anjou, unlike the big dikes co structed further upstream in later days, are not at monotonous: roads run along them, looking out ov the houses below to the fields and growing crops. In t rich valley, where hemp needed by factories near found particularly favourable conditions for its growt where William and Bon Chrétien pears used to be pr duced in abundance, small market-garden plots ha

most disappeared; the cultivation of fruit and vege-
.bles is now carried on in vast, open fields; the fertility
f the soil and the mild climate allow such produce as
ttuces, leeks and carrots, sown in autumn, to be
arvested the following spring. In the last few years
rain crops have replaced hemp.

On the left bank of the Loire, the real treasure of the
ountry is to be found on the chalky slopes of the Saumur
ills, both in the valley of the Loire and that of the
'houet; it is their vineyards. In the days of the Plan-
genets, the vine was cultivated over the whole of
njou, producing large quantities of wine for export to
ieir other dominions, Normandy and England; at a
.ter date, we can see in the illustrations of the *Très*
iches Heures du Duc de Berry grapes being harvested
round the Château of Saumur. In the eighteenth century
the Dutch were big buyers. Among the wines of the
Saumurois (Montsoreau, Turquant, Parnay, Saint-Cyr,
Brézé), wines of the 'tufa', both dry and sweet, the
bubbling Saumur stands apart; it was created in the nineteenth century, being brought to perfection in the cellars
of Saint-Hilaire-Saint-Florent following methods much
esteemed in Champagne.

Leaving Saumur in the direction of Gennes along the
left bank of the Loire, an enormous white tower rises
dominatingly over the township of Trèves. In Carolingian days this domain was called 'Clementiniacus' and
belonged to the Abbey of Saint-Aubin at Angers. If the
Chronicles of Saint-Florent are to be believed, the name of
Trèves (truces) was given in jest by Foulques Nerra,
Count of Anjou, then at war with the Lord of Saumur,
a vassal of the counts of Blois, who had asked for and

obtained a truce which was signed at this place. Foulques later built there, probably around 1020, a château to defend his possessions against the incursions of his neighbours. Many charters, particularly that of 1060, mention this château, which contained a church. In 1068, Foulques le Rechin destroyed the château and, probably, also the village, since he allowed the monks of Cunault to transfer both port and market to their own town. When a new château was built, however, Foulques insisted on port and market being returned; in 1101 he gave the place in fief to his steward, Geoffroy Foulcrade. In 1106, the latter granted to the Abbey of Saint-Aubin at Angers some land between the château, the Loire and a small stream, for the construction of a priory. The present church must have been begun about that time, but the dungeon-keep which we see today is neither that of Foulques Nerra nor of Foulques le Rechin.

During the thirteenth and fourteenth centuries, the domain of Trèves was in fact given in fief to various lords who took the title of counts of Trèves, before it was bought in 1417 by Robert le Maçon, Baron of Château-du-Loir, counsellor to the King of Sicily and Chancellor of Dauphin Charles. In 1420, the latter ceded to Robert le Maçon the right to levy tolls on all goods passing the château either by land or water. When Charles became king, Robert continued as Chancellor of the Kingdom and it was he who had a big château built; it was finished in 1435, but nothing of it now remains except the curious keep.

The lordship of Trèves then passed through the hands of various local families, notably the counts of Laval who, in 1642, were forced to agree to selling it t
Cardinal Richelieu; Richelieu quickly passed it on to hi
brother-in-law, the Marshal-Duke of Maillet-Brézé
The Great Condé, heir through his wife to the Maill
family, did homage to the king in 1681 for his barony o
Trèves, then a dependency of the royal château a
Saumur. A little later the château was bought by Joh
of Stapleton, an Irishman and one of the companions o
King James. Louis XV, wishing to settle that family i
France, in 1747, by letters patent, raised the barons o
Trèves to the status of counts. It was Stapleton wh
dismantled the château, except for the keep.

Robert le Maçon's château was built at the edge of
slope bordered by a small stream; the tufa is full o
underground passages. Some bits of walls and the pile
of the old entrance bridge survive, but the principal re
maining feature is the very well-preserved keep, with it
remarkable interior arrangements. It consists of a roun
tower on a talus alongside which, on the inner face of th
enceinte, is a polygonal mass of masonry; its walls, o
well-cut stones placed in regular rows, have opening
for cannons as well as arrow slits; the crenellated, poly
gonal top storey is surrounded with machicolation
decorated with trefoil arches. Inside there are severa
rooms with ogival vaults; the room on the second floo
is many-sided, having a middle portion with apses a
each end, the springers of the ribbing resting on impost
with carved escutcheons. This room has a vast fireplac
its lintel carved with a shield bearing fleurs-de-lis.

Robert le Maçon died in 1442 and his tomb has bee
preserved in the church at Trèves; he is represente
recumbent, his clerical dress beautifully draped, in a fla

Troglodyte
house at
Turquant

Modillions on the church at Cunault

backed niche roofed with intersecting arches and having a decoration of curled leaves.

The township of Cunault lies just outside Trèves. It was converted to Christianity in the fifth century by St Maxenceul, a disciple of St Martin, around whose tomb a small monastery was built in the tenth century. It is known that about the year 846 Charles the Bald granted the domain of Cunault to Count Vivien, Abbot of St Martin's, who at once passed it on to Hilbode, Abbot of Saint-Philibert-de-Grandlieu. The mortal remains of Philibert, formerly preserved at Grandlieu, were taken to Cunault, but Norsemen resumed their raids and the relics had to be removed, St Maxenceul's as well as St Philibert's; they eventually found refuge in the powerful Abbey of Tournus in Burgundy. This abbey became owner of the domain of Cunault and founded a priory there in the tenth century when the remains of St Maxenceul were returned to the place. Nothing remains of the first church built on the site. It was succeeded at the end of the eleventh century by an edifice of which the existing bell-tower is the last remaining trace. The rest of the church which we see today dates from the twelfth century; its construction spread over several periods, starting with the choir; the three western bays cannot have been completed before the very end of the century, or at the beginning of the thirteenth.

From the start, this priory received many donations, notably from the counts of Anjou and from the pilgrims who went there in search of a cure. The large number of pilgrims in the eleventh century made it necessary to build this immense church, far bigger than required by the needs of a small priory. In addition t the remains of St Maxenceul, two other relics wer shown for the veneration of the faithful: a ring repute to be the 'Holy Virgin's own wedding ring' and flask containing some of the dust from the grotto o Bethlehem.

The priory began to go downhill at the end of th Middle Ages; in 1741 it was abolished and the building given to the Angers seminary. The choir was decon secrated in 1749 by permission of the Conseil d'Etat an became a barn; in 1842, following a visit by Prospe Mérimée who brought the matter to the attention o Maine-et-Loire's General Council, it was decided t take over this part of the old church on behalf of th Commune, and a start was made on the work of restorin the whole building, which went on until 1886.

The Cunault church is one of the outstandin Romanesque buildings in Anjou and also one of th largest churches in France without a transept. It has choir of four bays with a rounded apse, surrounded b an ambulatory with three radiating chapels (the middl one has been destroyed) and a nave with aisles havin seven bays, two of which have parallel aisles on eithe side terminating in small apses, thus making a kind o transept. The three western bays of the nave and th aisles have Angevin ogival vaults; the remainder of th nave is roofed with a pointed cradle-vault, the aisles an the ambulatory with ribbed vaults.

The church owns an extraordinary collection c 240 capitals which enable one to follow both the stage of construction and the evolution of the styles of decora tion, and also sometimes to discover where the teams o

Fresco in the church at Cunault

rvers came from. The exterior of the oldest part of the urch, the bell-tower, which is now merged into the orth aisle, has all the characteristics of an eleventh-ntury building; the capitals are carved in archaic yle, like the one which reminds us that we are close to e Loire by its portrayal of a mermaid holding out a fish a boatman standing in his boat, a theme frequently und in La Vallée, for example at Saint-Maur and int-Aubin. The two upper storeys of the bell-tower, ith window openings under semicircular arches, are rmounted by an octagonal spire rising between four nall lanterns; these storeys, both inside and outside, ve the same decorative motifs as the big columns of e ground floor: battles between men and animals, ermaids, lions, horseshoes, a head in the process of ting long leaves. The capitals which form a con-uous band above the elegant piers of the apse portray ntastic animals facing each other, human-headed grif-ns, figures of people with wide-apart legs showing aces of colour, a warrior struggling with a monster.

Another series of capitals, probably carved when work as being done on the choir between 1130 and 1140, rry almost entirely non-religious scenes; there is an nnunciation, with David and Jesse on either side, a ortrayal of Christ carrying the Cross surrounded by ldiers with axes, and a very realistic Flagellation with a earded executioner brandishing his whip, but all the her scenes portray knights or crusaders: a knight in ain armour, fighting two Barbarians, standing before s caparisoned horse, sword and shield in hand; a night meeting a woman; a fight between a knight and monster; men riding on human-headed chimaeras;

monsters devouring each other. Some have thought that this set of carvings may be the work of a team of men who came from Saintonge where one can see, as at Cunault, a monstrous head devouring the shaft of a column.

In the central bays of the nave the motifs are purely decorative: foliage with caryatids, monsters or crouching human figures, all perfectly consistent with the Angevin style of decoration. The three western bays, the last to be built, have capitals portraying baskets of foliage, some of them closely resembling thirteenth-century crockets; depiction of subjects of religious nature is confined to the octagonal keystones, with scenes such as a Visitation surrounded by heads and busts of people, and to the base of the liernes, such as David playing the harp, St Michael slaying the dragon.

The western façade of the church is very simple; ground level, intersecting arches flank the doorwa under its semicircular arch; above, three windows wi intersecting arches rise to the level of the roof of th nave and aisles, the middle one having been filled, in th sixteenth century, with Flamboyant tracery. The tym panum of the doorway carries a representation of th Virgin in Glory seated on a fretwork throne, holdin the Child in front of her; a small figure of a donor knee at her feet; two censer-bearing angels of smaller siz stand on each side. This theme of the seated Virgin w much in vogue during the twelfth century, but certa details of the folds of the clothing suggest the possibili of a later attribution, to the beginning of the thirteen century. Finally, as at Candes, crenellations were adde to the top of the façade at the end of the Middle Age

Church at Cunault:
illar fresco and
ose decoration

Country-seat at Le Thoureil

The town of Gennes, a short way from Cunault, stands at the centre of one of the regions bordering the Loire where prehistory and history have left the most traces. The Commune has four dolmens and two menhirs in its territory; there are also very many reminders of the Romans: the remains of a vast amphitheatre, an aqueduct and two Roman roads. A Merovingian cemetery has also been found there.

The temples to Roman deities were succeeded by early churches, remodelled in the twelfth century, like Saint-Eusèbe and Saint-Vétérin. By the Middle Ages, this small centre had lost its former importance and become part of the barony – later county – of Trèves; the latter's law court, however, was transferred to Gennes in 1751, where it stayed until the Revolution. In the nineteenth century Gennes regained some of its importance because of its port on the Loire, where produce from the left bank was loaded, and also because of the construction of a suspension bridge uniting it with the important Commune of Les Rosiers on the right bank.

The Church of Saint-Eusèbe is very picturesque, standing on a steep slope overlooking the town from which the eye can range over the whole valley of the Loire; its site, however, exposed it to German bombardments in 1940, causing terrible havoc, now repaired. Some archaeologists have thought that parts of the church date from Merovingian days; one can, in fact, see big stretches of wall built of rows of cubic tufa blocks with regularly spaced, level insertions of three flat bricks placed horizontally, while the semicircular archway over one of the north doors consists of archstones alternating with bricks. These old parts were incorporated into a twelfth-century church whose nave was almo entirely rebuilt in the fifteenth century; the choir an the transept with its square tower are for the most pa of eleventh-century construction.

The other church, Saint-Vétérin, rises to the south c Gennes, on a hill above flood level, the site of th Merovingian cemetery. The place was once part of th domain of the Carolingian kings and in 845 was give to the neighbouring Abbey of Glanfeuil by Charles th Bald. This church contained the venerated body of S Vétérin, an unknown personage, whose mortal remai were conveyed to Burgundy at the time of the Gre Peregrination and were destroyed during the Wars c Religion. The church was ruined in 1770, but restored the nineteenth century. It consists of a single nave of tw bays, a transept with chapels in the two arms, a choir one bay, with a hemicycle beyond. The nave walls sho signs of old stonework, much like that at Saint-Eusèb part of which is Carolingian and part eleventh centur Most of the other parts of the church, among which a the carvings of foliage and water-plants on the capital date from the second half of the twelfth century.

Downstream from Gennes, on the left bank, the are many traces of prehistoric man in the form of do mens and menhirs. Charming villages are strung alor the banks of the river, like Le Thoureil with its pret houses about an eighteenth-century church, its curio thirteenth-century bell-tower decorated with blir arches. The building contains some works of art ster ming from the Abbey of Saint-Maur, whose ruins are short distance away. In the sixth century a monk, Maur, arrived at a place named 'Glanfolium' or Gla

Suspension bridge at Gennes,
framing the bell-tower of Saint-Eusèbe church

ult, where he founded one of the first French monasteries to adopt the Benedictine Rule, and built a small ermitage with a chapel, on the slope of the hill where a rcular Roman temple then existed, the ruins of which ere brought to light in 1898. He died there and was uried in the Merovingian chapel, on whose foundaons a church dedicated to him was built in the twelfth entury; the remains of his original sarcophagus are still ept in a crystal reliquary. The abbey was moved to the ank of the Loire. It was destroyed several times, sacked nd burnt by Norsemen and the English; it was bolished at the Revolution and most of its buildings isappeared. In 1890 Benedictine monks tried to bring it back to life, but abandoned it in 1903; today it is a school for junior members of the Assumptionist Order.

From the abbey church, a lovely Romanesque door now gives access to a modern chapel, inaugurated in 1955. The western gable of the Carolingian church has been preserved, its cross embellished with interlaced mouldings; but only a small wing of the big complex of the eighteenth-century buildings remains.

Along the left bank, the township of Blaison merits attention for the interesting fifteenth-century choir stalls in the old collegiate Church of Saint-Aubin, founded by Foulques Nerra in 1020. The church with its square bell-tower was built during the late twelfth or early thirteenth century. It was pillaged by the English in 1320, and the chapter was dissolved in 1780. Blaison was an important Angevin barony. Around the year 1040 the Bishop of Angers was feudal lord of Blaison. At the end of the eleventh century, Geoffroi de Blaison built a château there; in 1110 he became chancellor to Foulques V the Younger, Count of Anjou, who was crowned King of Jerusalem in 1131. But Geoffroi de Blaison became involved in a coalition against Foulques' successor Count Geoffroi le Bel, who demolished the château in 1147. It was soon rebuilt and became the birthplace of a very curious personage, Thibault de Blaison, a troubadour famous for his songs but also a fighting man. In 1206 and 1214, in fact, he is mentioned as being one of the guarantors of the truces concluded between the kings of France and the kings of England. In 1212 he took part in an expedition against the Moors in Spain and was present at the famous battle of Las Navas. Later, he is to be found in the French army which went with Simon de Montfort in the crusade against the Albingenses. He was even for some years steward of Poitou.

During the Hundred Years' War the English took Blaison, in 1320; the château was demolished and has not been rebuilt; only a dovecote and part of the main buildings remain.

To reach Angers by way of the left bank, one must cross the valley in which flow, on parallel courses, the Louet – a derivation of the Loire – the Loire itself with its wide arms running around inhabited islands, and finally the Authion in its straightened bed. There were bridges here as far back as the early Middle Ages and they are the reason for the existence of the curious tow on Ponts-de-Cé; hardly more than a long single stre with many fifteenth- and sixteenth-century houses, tw churches and the ruins of a château. Because of its stra tegic position, this town has played an important part i history; it has been the site of successive battles an sieges. It was fortified by the dukes of Anjou; th English took it during the Hundred Years' War in 136 and lost it again in 1438; in 1620, when Marie de Medi was fighting her son Louis XIII, she saw the army of he supporters defeated at this place; in 1651 the town wa captured from the Frondeurs; in 1793 it was seized b the Vendéan army but thereafter lost by them agair finally, it was heavily damaged during the Secon World War.

Between the Louet and the main arm of the Loire, th Church of Saint-Maurille rises over a blackish rock; stands at the boundary between the Parisian basin an the Armorican massif. From there, a bridge of twenty eight arches gives access to the island where King Ren often came to stay at the château whose fifteenth century polygonal keep now houses the gendarmeri Before going on to cross the Authion, one comes to th Church of Saint-Aubin, built in the twelfth century o a fief of the Abbey of Saint-Aubin at Angers; it wa damaged by bombardments in 1944. Behind it, a roa leads to Angers a few miles distant.

On the right bank, downstream from Les Rosie opposite Gennes, the small villages lining the bank, lik Saint-Mathurin, have kept their quays along the rive reminders of their former boating activities. Extendin back from the river is slate country; between Trélaz

Stalls in the church at Blaison

Slate-cutting at Trélazé

and Angers are four deep veins of schist. The slate quarries were being worked as far back as the twelfth century, but only by opencast mining; in the nineteenth century, operations became industrialized and shafts were sunk, providing access to work faces well underground; today skips are used to transport men and materials. The quarries provide employment for some five thousand 'underground' and 'surface' men; the latter are extremely skilful in their job of splitting the slate, and it is interesting to watch them reducing the great blocks of schist into thin, usable sheets of slate. The product of the quarries used to be transported by water and distributed on both sides of the Loire.

From Ponts-de-Cé one can see the town of Anger built some distance from the Loire valley on a schi spur overlooking the Maine, a river formed by th junction of the Sarthe, the Mayenne and the Loire little way upstream. At the time of the Roman conque the town, capital of a Gaulish tribe known as the 'Ande or 'Andecavi', became the city of 'Juliomagus' whe many monumental buildings were erected, includin baths, a circus, an amphitheatre; it became the foc point of a number of Roman roads. The Romans ma have encircled it with its first walls about the year A 300; traces of them have been found during excavation Although a definite date cannot be given, it was r

Old roof near Saint-Sulpice

ubt about the same time that Christianity came to
ıgers. A church must have existed there in the fifth
ıtury, probably outside the walls, perhaps on the site
the present cathedral, because it is known that a
ırch was burnt when Angers was taken by King
ıilderic in 471. There was already a bishopric in
gers at that time, and some of the prelates made their
ırk in history; for instance, St Maurille (died 453),
ıo had come from Milan and was a friend of St
ırtin and St Aubin; thanks to his support of King
ıildebert, he was able to unite in his own person the
ıctions of count and bishop. It was by the order of the
ne king that St Germain, Bishop of Paris, came to
ınd an abbey at Angers, the first abbey in the whole
Anjou, which became known as the Abbey of Saint-
ıbin. A second abbey was founded in that town a
le later, probably by Clovis II. In 835 Louis the Pious
ıewed the privileges of the cathedral church and
ınted to the bishop the right to own three boats,
empt from all tolls and taxes, on the Loire and its
butaries.

As the population increased, it spread outside the
llo-Roman enclosure, and Charles the Bald sur-
ınded the town with a larger wall. In 853, however,
ɔrsemen occupied and pillaged Angers; in the follow-
; year, there was another raid, and renewed pillage
d raids continued for more than ten years; in 872 the
ɔrsemen occupied the town but were dislodged by
arles the Bald the year after; from 877 to 882, they
ied an annual tribute; their last raid took place in 903.
then a dynasty of counts had established themselves
Anjou. The townships which had grown up outside

Buttress towers,
Château of Angers

the walls of the town around the churches and abbeys were re-established; on the other side of the Maine, new townships came into being around the new Abbeys of Notre-Dame-de-la-Charité or Ronceray and Saint-Nicolas, founded around 1020 by Foulques Nerra and his wife.

The monasteries sustained a certain level of intellectual life; calligraphers, who had studied at the famous school of Tours, produced beautiful manuscripts; the bishopric founded a school in the eleventh century; at the same time work on the cathedral was continuing, the architect for the nave being Hubert of Vendôme, who had come from Marmoutier before going on to Nantes; the nave, incidentally, was transformed by Normand de Doué during the Gothic period.

In 1155 the House of Anjou ascended the throne of England in the person of Henry II Plantagenet, who nevertheless paid frequent visits to Angers and continued his benefactions to the city where he founded the hospital of Saint John. His successors made only brief visits and, consequently, no problems arose when Anjou became part of the domains of the kings of France in 1214 after the victory of Philippe Auguste over John Lackland. Shortly thereafter, Angers was given in appanage together with Anjou and continued its development. King St Louis turned the château into an imposing fortress and surrounded the city and its suburbs with a third wall, which disappeared only at the beginning of the nineteenth century. The bishops continued work on the cathedral; the schools became active again and in 1229 Parisian students took refuge at Angers after arguments with the Provost of Paris. Thereafter, in 1364, at

Details from the Apocalypse tapestry in the Château of Angers

the request of Duke Louis I, the schools became a uni versity with privileges similar to those enjoyed by th university of Orléans; the three faculties were legall created in 1432 by Pope Eugenius IV; the students wer divided into six 'nations': Anjou, Brittany, Main Normandy, Aquitaine and France (i.e. Ile-de-France The university became very famous, especially for i law school, which in the sixteenth century produced group of excellent jurists, such as Jean Bodin.

The dukes of Anjou became the centre of a group c distinguished people; the last duke, King René, was him self a painter and writer as well as patron and friend c artists.

In 1480, Anjou became finally united with the Crow of France; the town of Angers received a charter and citizen organization grew up, with a mayor, aldermen councillors, magistrates, etc. These citizens built beaut ful mansions, many of which still exist. The poe Joachim du Bellay sang of Anjou and the 'Gaulish River

During the Wars of Religion and the Fronde ther was trouble in Angers. In the seventeenth and eighteent centuries, the university did not have the same influenc as in the fifteenth century because its professors re mained faithful to the teachings of the Scholastics whic the Oratorians were tearing to pieces. In 1686 a new cultural centre was nevertheless created by letters paten from Louis XIV, namely the Literary Academy, whic survived until the Revolution. In 1793 both academ and university disappeared. The country suffered great during the Vendée peasants' rising; in 1793 the latt marched against Angers and occupied it in the mont of June, only to be thrown out in December. In 181

Following pages:
façade of 'Adam's House' at Angers

t the end of the Napoleonic Wars, Angers was occupied y five thousand Prussians.

During the nineteenth century Angers became, ccording to the expression used by the geographer ean Brunhes, 'a town animating a hybrid province nade of complementary regions'. It was not only an ndustrial town, with slate quarries, hemp mills and istilleries, but also a floricultural town surrounded by ose and nursery gardens, with the Arboretum and the ruit Garden. From 1875 Angers began again to be an ntellectual centre with the creation, on the initiative f Mgr Freppel, of the Catholic University of the West, o which other teaching establishments were later added.

In the twentieth century, however, Angers once more had to endure occupation by foreigners and to suffer considerable damage; during the Second World War more than 2,500 buildings were hit, 544 being completely destroyed during May and June 1940 and in 1944. Despite its centuries of destruction, Angers is still rich in old buildings – religious, civic and military.

The Cathedral of Saint-Maurice, built in the twelfth century and remodelled in the thirteenth and fifteenth, is a magnificent edifice; despite nineteenth-century alterations, the façade is most imposing. Inside, the three bays of the nave are roofed with very high ogival vaults and the windows have precious twelfth-century stained

'Luxury' from the façade of 'Adam's House' at Angers

Carved corbel of the façade of 'Adam's House' at Angers

glass as well as some dating from the thirteenth and fifteenth centuries.

The purest Angevin style of construction, however, is to be found in the Church of Saint-Sergius. This choir consists of three naves of four bays each, separated by tall, elegant columns; the very lovely vaults are truly typical; part of the transept goes back to the eleventh century, and the triple nave dates from the fifteenth.

Trinity church, formerly a dependency of the Ronceray abbey, was built during the second half of the twelfth century; its single nave of seven bays is roofed with vaults of Norman influence.

One of the oldest monuments of Angers is the old Saint-Martin's church; it had been scheduled for demolition but was saved at the beginning of the twentieth century by the efforts of learned archaeologists. A Merovingian oratory existed on this site, followed by a Carolingian church, which was destroyed by Norsemen; Foulques Nerra rebuilt it and enlarged it; the choir was added at the end of the twelfth century, with a graceful chapel in the Angevin style.

Finally, there are the remains of the Abbey of Saint-Aubin; they are admirably preserved at the Prefecture, especially the twelfth-century Romanesque arches with their remarkable decorative carvings.

Among the non-religious buildings, the old hospital of Saint John, now an archaeological museum, is one of the most beautiful examples of this kind of architecture in France, with its great hall for patients, its cloister and its storehouses. The long hall consists of three naves of equal height, each with eight bays; fourteen monolithic columns, together with the columns adjoining e walls, carry the remarkable Angevin vaults; a little stance away, Saint John's storehouse, a two-storey ıilding of the same period, served as cellar and store-om; the ground floor, cut into the slate-bearing hist, is now the Anjou Wine Museum, containing ine-presses and wine-growers' tools.

Angers also has some fifteenth- and sixteenth-century ıildings. The best known of the wood-and-brick ouses is 'Adam's House', formerly called 'Tree of Life'; though the Adam-and-Eve group has been destroyed, e wooden consoles supporting the moulded, dragon-rved beams are very realistically carved with charming tle human figures, like the bagpipe player or the two vers. The wooden post supporting the different oreys of the old Simon Poisson pharmacy, dating om 1582, are carved with tall human figures portray-g Magnificence, Science, Friendship and Generosity. f the stone buildings, many new museums housing ecious collections, the Barrault and Pincé mansions erit more detailed consideration. At the end of the teenth century, Olivier Barrault, Treasurer of Brit-ny and Mayor of Angers, had this elegant dwelling ıilt 'to lodge and house his family and to receive in fitting manner his friends and other worthy persons', d it was indeed there that distinguished personages ssing through Angers in the sixteenth and seventeenth centuries used to stay, including Cesare Borgia, Mary Stuart and Marie de Medici. Between 1523 and 1535, Jean de Pincé, the criminal lieutenant of the Seneschal of Anjou, also built a mansion which is a remarkable example of transitional architecture.

Finally, the dark mass of the Château of Angers, in its ring of schist walls, looks down on the left bank of the Maine. Dating for the most part from the thirteenth century, it consists of a vast enclosure with seventeen towers. It took ten years to build, from 1230 to 1240; many of the additions – the chapel and the Royal Lodge – are the works of the dukes of Anjou; King René planted a garden in which he installed menageries and aviaries. In 1585 the château just missed being razed to the ground; fortunately, only the tower roofs were demolished. Successively a fortress, a State prison, a barracks and an arsenal, the château became the property of the State only in 1857; but it still had not been evacuated by the eve of the Second World War, and the German army used it as a munitions depot. Finally, in 1945, the Direction-Générale des Beaux-Arts began the work of restoring this complex monument; between 1952 and 1954, a special edifice was constructed to house and exhibit the famous tapestry of the Apocalypse, an extraordinary piece of work woven between 1377 and 1384 by Nicolas Bataille for Louis I of Anjou.

The Loire of the Sea

aving Angers, the river Maine continues on its way to e Loire as far as the well-named village of Bouche- aine, running between lovely hills on its right and t fields on its left; nowadays it joins the Loire a little rther downstream opposite the village of La Pointe. om this point onwards the Loire looks quite different; is the Loire of Brittany, flowing into the sea. It is still ll of islands, but they are less unstable than those stream and often cling to great masses of primary ystalline rock, as at Béhuard; other vertical extrusions similar rock are to be seen along the banks, for ample Roche-Bécherelle and Roche-aux-Moines. On is maritime reach of the Loire there is an increasingly ely river traffic. Between Nantes and Bouchemaine ods are carried in barges of an average capacity of o tons; in 1968, on this section of the river, some ,000 barge loads were carried, totalling more than 300,000 tons of building materials and manufactured oducts, as well as 117,000 tons of petroleum products. ne barges naturally serve the many small river ports of is section. Investigations are now under way regarding e possibility of extending this traffic upstream from ouchemaine as far as the junction with the Vienne, king in Saumur on the way.

On the right bank of the Loire stands the old town- ip of Savennières, the 'Vicus Saponaria', which was d waste first by Bretons and then several times by orsemen in 840 and 912; it was the site of a priory of e Saint-Sergius Abbey at Angers and possesses an tremely interesting church; the west front and the uth side of the single nave can be traced back to the nth century, although some archaeologists are doubt- ful about classing it as one of the oldest churches in Anjou. Horizontal rows of flat stones and bricks, placed either flat or in herring-bone pattern, are inserted into the fine masonry of the walls; the east end of the church is a twelfth-century Romanesque choir in tufa stone.

Opposite Savennières, on a long island in the middle of the river, stands a curious church, set on a naked rock, which has long served as a landmark for the boatmen of the Loire. Tradition has it that in Gaulish days a sanctuary stood on this spot, dedicated to the cult of a tutelary deity of sailors, in place of which St Maurille substituted the veneration of the Virgin during his proselytizing sermons in the fifth century. About the middle of the eleventh century, the group of small islands, today united into a single large one, was given in fief by Geoffroy Martel, Count of Anjou to a knight of Breton origin named Béhuard who at his death left them to the Abbey of Saint-Nicolas at Angers. On one of these islands stands 'the rock, my house and the chapel' as well as 'the fisheries, the canal and the mill'. In the Middle Ages a pilgrimage developed; in 1434 the English, then in occupation of the province of Maine, are recorded as having issued to pilgrims from Sillé-le-Guillaume passes for travel to the sanctuary of Béhuard. In 1453, Dauphin Louis, the future Louis XI, in danger while navigating the Charente, invoked the help of Notre-Dame-de-Béhuard and was saved. During his lifetime he paid some twenty visits to the chapel, which he rebuilt in 1469. Thereafter, the pilgrimages slowed down because of the Wars of Religion and pillaging habits of the Ligueurs; they resumed only in 1870; nowadays, pilgrims flock to this tiny sanctuary each

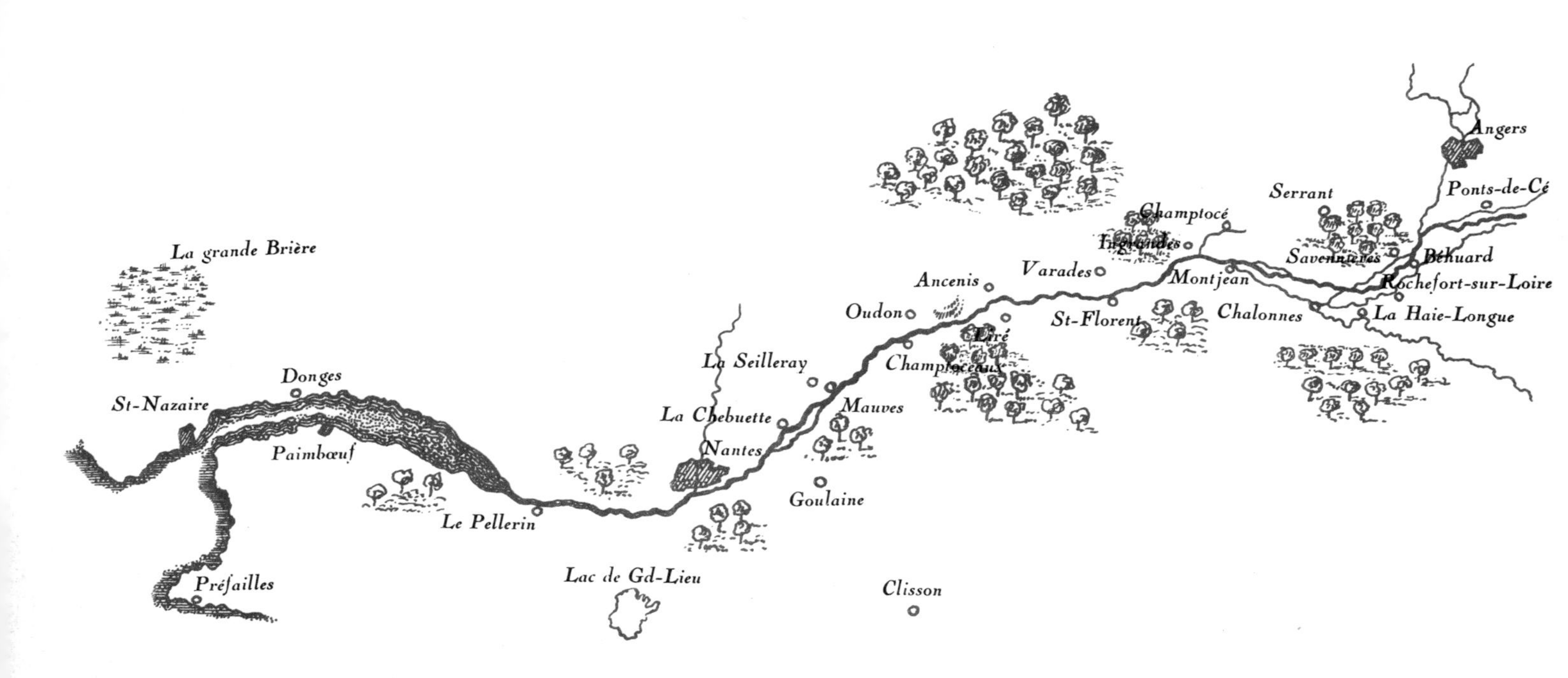

year on the eighth of September; it has a vaulted wooden roof and lovely fifteenth-century stained glass.

The famous vineyard of 'Coulée de Serrant' belongs to the Commune of Savennières; its slatey soil produces one of the best wines of Anjou, sweet and fragrant. Not far from the Loire, in the middle of this vineyard, are to be seen the ruins of the Château of Roche-aux-Moines, to which John Lackland laid siege in 1214 but was unable to take because of the arrival of an army under the command of Louis, son of Philippe Auguste; the château was destroyed during the League troubles. As the crow flies, the domain of Serrant lies just a few miles from the Loire; in the fifteenth and sixteenth centuries it belonged to the Brie family, and in 1481 Ponthus de Brie began to build a château with ramparts and drawbridge which his descendants progressively replaced by the edifice which we see today. The left wing with its beautiful straight staircase recalling the one at Azay-le-Rideau, was finished only at the time ‹ the death of Charles de Brie. The new owners, tl Bautru family, began to work on it in 1636 and con pleted the chapel, which contains the tomb of Nicol Bautru, Marquis of Vaubrun, Lieutenant-General ‹ the Royal Armies, killed in battle at Altenheim in 167 The tomb was ordered in 1677, to be made to the pla of the painter Charles le Brun, but it was not installe until 1704. On a background of black marble, betwe two Corinthian pilasters, stands a Victory carved l Colignon, looking down on a sarcophagus where tl statue of the Marquis of Vaubrun lies on a heap ‹ weapons and flags while the Marchioness kneels besi him, draped in a large cloak. The statues are the work ‹ Antoine Coysevox, who also did the bas-relief repr senting the battle of Altenheim. In 1730 the domain Serrant was bought by Jack Walsh, grandson of tl English naval captain who took King James to Franc

Notre-Dame chapel,
Béhuard

Following pages:
country-seat on the
banks of the Loire
at Saint-Mathurin

In March 1755, Louis XV made Serrant an earldom and the domain subsequently passed into the ownership of the de la Trémoille family.

The château, which possesses a rich collection of works of art, consists of a main body and two angled wings; the position of the central stairway is peculiar; two pavilions at the end of the wings complete the square. The château is surrounded by gardens and a balustraded terrace projects into a broad expanse of water. The ruins appearing opposite Savennières on the slope above the left bank are those of the castle of Rochefort-sur-Loire; it was rebuilt several times after the twelfth century, and at the end of the sixteenth it became a den of Ligueurs, and Henry IV had to buy it from them since he was unable to take it by assault; he had it immediately dismantled.

Downstream from Rochefort the valley widens and the river splits into many arms which flow past low, damp islands bordered with willows and ash trees; wide communal pastures alternate with fields of wheat, vegetables and hemp. As far as Chalonnes, the Angevin corniche road runs along under steeply sloping hills; at their feet flows the Louet, a true arm of the Loire, which it accompanies from Ponts-de-Cé until it joins the Layon near Chalonnes. On this corniche, in the hamlet of Haie-Longue, stands a monument to an Angevin pioneer of aviation who carried out his first flights at that place in 1908.

Chalonnes, 'Colonia', was a Gallo-Roman villa where St Maurille, before becoming Bishop of Angers, reputedly founded a monastery and built a church above the remains of a pagan temple. The Church of Saint-Maurille, heavily damaged in June 1940, has a twelfth-century choir roofed with a dome on pendentives, and aisles ending in chapels with Angevin vaults. The feudal château belonged to bishops of Angers and was built on a rock at the side of the Loire; at one time a bridge connected it with an island in the river.

According to a charter of Charles the Bald dated 849, the Layon, which runs into the Loire at Chalonnes, used to be the boundary between the lands of the 'Andecavi' and those of the 'Pictavi'. In the last part of its course, between Beaulieu and Aubin-de-Luigné, this tiny river has dug a picturesque corridor through ancient rock formations; winding along in an asymmetrical valley, it has on its right the continuing chalky escarpments of Anjou, and on its left the gentle slopes of the Mauges tableland, the last projection of the Armorican massif. The lower slopes of this valley produce some of the most famous wines of the Layon: Beaulieu, Rablay, Thouarcé. The 'chenin' and 'pineau' grapes are lovingly tended; many methods are used for determining the moment when the 'noble rot' has reached the stage where the grapes should be cut; and the wine thus obtained, according to real wine-lovers, 'leaves on the tongue a delicate taste resembling a bowl of fruit with a peacock's tail' (a wine with a remarkable wealth and range of aftertaste).

Opposite Montjean, which also produces good wine on its slopes, on the right bank of the river beyond a wide stretch of water or *boire*, are the extensive ruins of a large château destroyed during the Wars of Religion, whose owner in the fifteenth century committed some detestable crimes; it is the Château of Champtocé, one

Terrace and pond,
Château of Serrant

Le Louet from the corniche
at La Haie-Longue

of the oldest lordships in Anjou. About the year 1200, Champtocé became the property of the House of Craon through the marriage of Tiphaine de Champtocé, nicknamed 'The Eel', to Maurice de Craon, and it remained in the hands of the lords of Craon until the end of the fourteenth century when Marie de Craon took it as her dowry to Guy de Laval. Their son was the famous Gilles de Retz, faithful companion of Joan of Arc and Marshal of France during the reign of Charles VII, at whose coronation he was present. Around 1432, however, he gave up his military career and lived shut up in his Châteaux of Champtocé, Machecoul, Tiffauges and others where he devoted himself to the practice of sorcery, alchemy and black magic. He surrounded himself with sorcerers, some of whom he even brought from Italy, vowing himself to Satan and sacrificing children. He was arrested by order of the king and brought before a tribunal consisting of the chief magistrates of Brittany, Pierre de l'Hospital, the Bishop of Nantes, Jean de Malestroit, and the Inquisitor Jean Blouyn. The man, often known as the 'Blue-Beard of Nantes', was sentenced to be burnt alive and was so put to death on 23 December 1440 at Nantes, on the plain of Biesse in the middle of the Loire.

The *boire* of Champtocé runs into the Loire at Ingrandes where formerly a great stone marked the boundary between Anjou and Brittany. Ingrandes is also the western limit of cultivation of the Angevin 'pineau' grape; downstream, and in the whole of the region of Nantes, two kinds of white grape are predominantly grown: the 'gros plant' and the 'muscadet', the latter imparting a musky taste to its wine. The

The Loire below
Saint-Florent-le-Vieil

Following pages:
view of Champtoceaux

method of cultivation also differs; there are fewer small landowners than in Anjou and more tenant farmers. Ingrandes, a stronghold which was dismantled after the Wars of Religion, was a dependency of the counts of Anjou and was, like Champtocé, the scene of some of Gilles de Retz' dreadful activities. The township still has some sixteenth-century houses, principally the Hôtel de la Croix-de-Lorraine, which Gilles de Retz used to visit, and the Hôtel du Grand Louis, where Louis XIV stayed.

The Loire then runs southwest as far as Saint-Florent-le-Vieil on its left bank, where a hermit named Florent came to stay in the fourth century in a grotto at the top of a hill called Mount Glonne. Naturally, numerous legends grew up about him; he is said to have delivered the region from the ravages of a fearsome dragon and to have lived to be 123 years old. After his death an abbey was founded by his disciples, who in 824 adopted the Benedictine Rule. Charlemagne and Louis the Pious showered benefits on it, but soon the threat of raiding Norsemen forced the monks to try to find a safe place for the relics of St Florent, which thus began their peregrinations. And the Norsemen, indeed, from their base on the big island at the foot of Mount Glonne, came several times to sack the monastery, notably in 833, 866 and 875. In 950 the community of monks started up again, sharing their abbot with the monks of Saint-Florent-de-Saumur. Bit by bit a village grew up around the abbey. In 1793, Saint-Florent became one of the theatres of the Vendée war. In the month of March six thousand peasants occupied the village and stayed there for one month; in October, after the battle of

Cholet, the defeated Vendéan army fell back on Saint-Florent on their way to Varades on the other side of the river. They had with them five thousand Republican prisoners, all of whom they were on the point of shooting, being unable to take them over the Loire, when one of their leaders, Bonchamps, who was mortally wounded, ordered them to desist; the prisoners were saved, but Bonchamps died on a boat in the middle of the river. His tomb stands in the Church of Saint-Florent: it is a statue in white marble, by David of Angers, and it portrays Bonchamps at the moment when he spoke the words, 'Spare the prisoners'.

There used to be a church at Varades, a dependency of the Abbey of Marmoutiers, and the record shows that a fifteenth-century lord of Varades granted exemption from payment of tolls to Marmoutier goods travelling on the river.

The town of Ancenis rises in an amphitheatre abov its port; it is surrounded by hillsides covered witl vineyards. In the tenth century, in the year 982, th Countess of Nantes built a château at this place as protection against the counts of Anjou, and one of ther tried unsuccessfully to take it by assault in 987. However, Henry II, King of England, after making himsel master of part of Brittany, took Ancenis, fortified it an entrusted it to Maurice de Craon. John Lackland, on hi last expedition to the banks of the Loire, managed t recapture Ancenis as well as Oudon, from which h ravaged the surrounding country; but in 1213, Geoffro d'Ancenis took the place again. Thereafter Anceni became successively the property of the Houses o Brittany, Rochefort, Mercœur, etc. In the reign o Louis XI the town resisted the royal troops in 1468, bu in the month of September Francis II, Duke of Brittany

Breakwater in the Loire

reed to sign a treaty with the king at Ancenis. In 1488 e royal army under the command of La Trémoille ized Ancenis and burnt it; in 1490 Duchess Anne (of rittany), having become Queen of France, had the âteau pulled down; the fortifications were repaired in e next century, but in 1599 Henry IV had them smantled again. All that remains today of the fifteenth-ntury château is a fortified doorway between two ormous, machicolated towers and an edifice erected 1535 by an Angevin architect, Jean de l'Espine; some venteenth-century buildings also survive.

South of Ancenis, on the right bank of the Loire, lies small village which claims the honour of being the rthplace of a poet of the Angevin Renaissance, achim du Bellay. He was born in 1522 in the manor La Tourmelière, in the parish of Liré. The manor was irnt by the Blues in 1792 and all that remains of it is a bit of ivy-covered wall. In his collection of poems entitled *Regrets*, the poet sang of his village and his 'poor house, to me worth more than a province', the bluish slates and the 'sweet softness' of Anjou.

The rocky hills beside the Loire between Liré and Champtoceaux are magnificently wooded with cedar, chestnut and walnut trees. The township of Champtoceaux itself rises on a wooded height affording a wide view over the valley from Saint-Florent as far as the town of Nantes. Champtoceaux and its château played an important part in all the wars of the Middle Ages, waged for the possession of Brittany between the counts of Anjou and the dukes of Brittany and later between the Houses of Blois and de Montfort after the death of Duke Jean III of Brittany in 1363. Having been a dependency of the counts of Anjou in the eleventh century, the lordship of Champtoceaux passed into the

Preceding pages:
sunset at La Chebuette

Oudon: remains of the Châte

hands of the dukes of Brittany, but in 1173 the army of Henry II of England came and retook it. In the fourteenth century, despite the sieges it had undergone, the Château of Champtoceaux was a redoubtable, well-garrisoned fortress. When King Philip of Valois came out in favour of the Count of Blois, the Duke of Normandy assembled an army at Angers, crossed the Loire at Ancenis and laid siege to Champtoceaux, which was held on behalf of Count de Montfort. A long siege ensued and the defenders were defeated only by the use of siege artillery; the garrison finally surrendered and the château was taken over by the Count of Blois' men who set to and repaired its defences.

Marguerite de Clisson came to live in retirement at Champtoceaux in 1420 with her son Oliver, Count of Blois; she was the daughter of Constable Olivier de Clisson and widow of the Count of Penthiève. Her son went to pay his respects to Duke Jean V, then holding court at Nantes, and to invite him to visit the Countess of Penthièvre. The duke and his suite started on their journey on 12 February but were attacked by men from Blois; the duke was captured and shut up in a tower of the castle at Champtoceaux, where he was held prisoner for several months. The duchess, however, called on her barons to take up the fight, and they laid waste the lands of the Penthièvre family and besieged the château. The duke was finally set free, and this latest event in the struggle between the Houses of Blois and de Montfort ended with the destruction of both the town and the Château of Champtoceaux. In the vast park in which the modern château stands, there are still some ivy-covered bits of walls, all that remains of the old fortress.

On the right bank opposite Champtoceaux is t small town of Oudon amidst its vineyards, where magnificent octagonal fifteenth-century keep stan amid ruins of a thirteenth-century château; built black slate, with white quoins, it has a spiral staircase c in the thickness of the walls. The lordship of the pla belonged for more than two centuries to the Malestr family, of which two brothers, during the reign François I, were convicted of forging money a condemned to death; the château was confiscated a sold.

Between Champtoceaux and Oudon the Loi narrows to flow through wide outcrops of grani which cut up its banks into steep promontories, and it from above a high granite crag that the town of Mauv looks down on the Loire; the nearby, higher hill Saint-Clément is the site of an old Roman villa. On bo banks of the river, among ruins of old châteaux, the are many pleasant mansions, both old and modern, su as the Château of Clairmont on the right bank, co structed on the site of the Abbey of Mont-Clair, whi was destroyed by Norsemen in 843, and also t Château of La Varenne on the left bank, where t Loire is joined by the Divatte. The hinterlands betwe the Loire and the Erdre, on the one hand, and the Loi and the Nantes Sèvre, on the other, are very similar.

A few miles from Mauves rises the magnifice Château of La Seilleray, built on a height overlooki the Seil. In 1671, a certain M. d'Harouis, counsellor the Breton parliament and Provincial Treasure General, bought the domain with its feudal manc house and started at once to have the present châte

Pediment in the courtyard, Château of La Seilleray

built to plans of François Mansard. It consists of a hug central portion of three storeys and two wings of th same height joined to each other by railings enclosin the main courtyard. The façade of the middle bloc carries a triangular pediment on two pilasters topped b urns; a very simple gallery carried on arches leads to chapel which is, like the main staircase, abundantl gilded. Outside, a garden laid out by Le Nôtre ends i an immense lawn sloping gently up to a combination c pergolas and alleys planted with hornbeams. Far off ar the valley and the hills of Loroux-Bottereau, overlook ing the nature reserve of the Goulaine marshes. Madam de Sévigné, a first cousin of M. d'Harouis' wife, Marie Madeleine de Coulanges, visited the château. A portra of the Marchioness dressed as Diana the Huntress, th costume in which she danced a quadrille while Louis XI looked on, hangs in her bedroom; several of her lette are dated from La Seilleray. In addition to some lovel tapestries, the picture gallery of the château contains a important collection of eighteenth-century painting In the garden of La Seilleray is the place where deputation from the town of Nantes came to offe Henry IV the silver keys of the town, together wit bread and wine, and presents for his suite: Gabriel d'Estrées was given 'gloves perfumed with ambergri sugarcoated nuts and tame canaries in a gilded cage'.

A short distance from Loroux on the other side of th river stands the Château of Goulaine, restored by th owner in 1920. In the ninth or tenth century a mano house stood on this site, and the House of Goulaine w already well known. In 1184, Alphonse de Goulain was chosen to arbitrate in a dispute between the King c

The banks of the
Loire at Mauves

France, Philippe Auguste, and the King of England, Henry II. As a reward for his services he was granted the right to carry armorial bearings, half French and half English, with the device 'I grant crowns to the one and the other'. With the passing of the years the château was reconstructed several times and the domain of Goulaine, always owned by the same family, was made into a marquisate in 1621 in favour of Gabriel de Goulaine. The existing edifice, surrounded by wide moats and built close to the marshes, consists of a large, fifteenth-century main block of buildings with wide windows and a line of dormer windows standing out of the steep roofs; on one side is the chapel and on the other the stables built during the reign of Louis XIII. Inside, the first-floor rooms are decorated in the seventeenth-century style, with painted and gilded ceilings and hangings of cordovan leather; the armorial bearings of the family are part of the decoration. The old defensive walls which have survived have a carving above one of the doors of a woman's head and shoulders, helmeted and with a dagger pointed towards her heart; some historians have interpreted this carving in a way which is very dramatic, if not based on historical fact: the daughter of a lord of Goulaine, left alone at the château with a few men while her father went to harry the English, found herself besieged by the latter and tried to hold out; but the garrison was soon on the point of being forced to surrender. The young lady preferred to put an end to her life rather than fall into enemy hands but, just when she was about to put her decision into effect, she saw her father's men, from the top of the château, as they routed the enemy.

The Goulaine marshes lie close to the château: like La Brière or the lake at Grand-Lieu, they have been formed by progressive filling in of depressions existing in geological times; for the local inhabitants they provide peat and supplies of bedding for their animals. Eels and frogs abound and waterfowl find cover there. These marshes, like others in the region, drain into the Loire through *acheneaux*. The Goulaine *acheneau* joins the river below the village of La Basse-Goulaine, close to Saint-Sébastien, where the right bank levee comes to an end and where the noises of the town of Nantes are audible. The Loire valley here gives place to the estuary; the highest tides used to make themselves felt well up-stream from Oudon but, since regulatory mechanisms were constructed in the nineteenth century, they do not nowadays reach higher than Mauves, where the salt water ceases.

Nantes is now the regional capital of the Loire country comprising the Departments of Loire-Atlantique, Vendée, Maine-et-Loire, Mayenne and Sarthe; it has a long history as a capital city. When the Romans reached thi region they found a Gaulish tribe living there, the Namnetes, one of the five tribes of the Armorican peninsula. A Roman town known as 'Condovincum grew up on a site above flood level, at the junction of the Loire and the Erdre, with a port on the river bank 'Portus Namnetum'. In the fourth century a square enceinte, whose traces can be seen in the existing château, was built round the by then very flourishing Gallo-Roman town. Christianity seems to have come to

Fishing boat
at La Chebuette

Seventeenth-century house at Nantes: mascaron on the façade

the region in the fourth century, with St Clair; around the year 304 two brothers named Donatien and Rogatien, respectively, known as the 'Youths of Nantes', suffered martyrdom there. No cathedral church, however, existed before the middle of the sixth century; the first one was consecrated only in 586 by St Felix whom King Clotaire installed as bishop, after chasing out the Bretons in 560. Tradition attributes to this bishop the execution of important works, notably the deepening of an arm of the Loire between the plain of Mauves and Gloriette island to provide easier access to the river for the townsfolk. After a period about which little is known, Norsemen settled in the isle of Noirmoutier and succeeded, thanks to treachery, in seizing and pillaging the city about the year 843, massacring the bishop and all the faithful. They returned in 853 and made their headquarters on the isle of Biesse in the river. In 877 Charles the Bald retook the city and built a new enceinte; despite this, the city was unable to fight off a fresh attack by Norsemen in 919, in which the cathedral was set on fire and the place completely sacked. For twenty years it lay in a state of ruin until the Norsemen were forced to evacuate the Loire islands by Alain Barbetort, who built the first château around 940.

After Alain Barbetort's death in 952, the state of anarchy returned while the counts of Nantes and of Rennes fought over the sovereignty of Brittany. Then, Nantes was for a time a dependency of the counts of Anjou; in 1207, Guy de Thours, husband of Duchess Constance, had a large edifice built outside of and at an angle to the Gallo-Roman enclosure, named the 'Château of the New Tower', whose foundations were rediscovered during excavations in 1922. This châtea was extended and completed by Pierre de Dreux whom in 1223, Philippe Auguste invested with the duchy o Brittany; he chose Nantes as his capital. The followin year the city beat off an attack by John Lackland. Pierr de Dreux abdicated in 1237 in favour of his son, Jean the Red, and the latter continued to enlarge the châtea during the fifty years he reigned over the duchy.

Seaborne commerce became ever more extensive and both port and city slowly extended downstream. I the thirteenth century the bishop, who shared with th duke and the count the income from a tax on importe goods, acquired the fief of La Fosse in order to construc a deep-water seaport. In the fourteenth and fifteent centuries the principal seaport of the region was in th Bourgneuf bay, where both sailors from the north an the riverine population of the Loire came to find salt The riverine merchant community dominated th economic life of Nantes, based mainly on trade of win and spirits; but some merchants from Hanseatic town and a small colony of Spaniards also settled in the city

At the end of the fourteenth century and during th whole of the fifteenth, the dukes of Brittany made th château their residence. Taking advantage of a perio of peace and prosperity, Duke Jean V decided to replac the old Romanesque cathedral with a larger and mor beautiful building; in April 1434 he laid the first ston of a building which was destined to remain under con struction for more than four hundred years. François II on becoming duke in 1459, undertook the complet reconstruction of the château in 1466; only some mino alterations were made to the defences by Duke Mercœu

Nautical motif on the walls
of the Château of Nantes

t the end of the sixteenth century. In 1460, François II btained from Pope Pius II authority to found a niversity having the same privileges as that of Orléans. The wedding of François II and Marguerite de Foix took lace at the château, and their daughter Anne was born here in 1476. On the death of her father, whose tomb vas originally placed in the Carmelite church but is now n the cathedral, Anne became Duchess of Brittany in 488. In the month of December 1491, Duchess Anne vas married to Charles VIII at Langeais, taking the luchy of Brittany to him as her dowry. The University of Nantes, which was in a somewhat decayed state, was given assistance. King Charles died in 1498; the luchess retired to her Château of Nantes where, in June 499, she was married to Louis XII.

The seaborne trade of Nantes began to increase in the ixteenth century; from a port exporting wine it became port importing precious metals, raw sugar, tobacco nd spices from the West Indies, Africa and India. The rincipal merchants in the sixteenth century were the Spaniards, in the seventeenth the Dutch and many other ationalities. The city's population increased and spread vestwards outside the encircling walls; a new town grew up at La Fosse. From the Revocation of the Edict of Nantes in 1685 until the Revolution, Nantes took ull advantage of its privileged situation with regard to he West Indies. Refineries, born of the sugar trade, vere built at the end of the seventeenth century and the lave trade, too, brought large profits to shipowners. The apogee of Nantes' commercial activity under the *Ancien Régime* was reached in the eighteenth century. The city embellished itself; newly enriched shipowners

Exterior walls, Château of Nante

had beautiful mansions built; the enceinte walls were replaced with tree-covered courtyards. New industries began to grow in the suburbs.

The Revolution and the Empire dealt a terrible blow to Nantes' trade. Long-distance sea traffic, which in 1790 accounted for nearly 100,000 tons, had fallen to barely 18,000 tons by 1802. Coastal trade had become impossible and the ships stayed in port. The loss of Louisiana and the abolition of the slave trade deprived the trade of its sources. Nantes had welcomed the Revolution, but experienced in 1793 four months of terror – guillotine and drownings – instituted by the sinister Carrier, who came to the city as the envoy of the Committee of Public Safety. At the same time Nantes had to fight the Vendéans, repelling an attack in 1793, during which Cathelineau was killed; Charette was shot in Nantes in 1796.

After 1815, progressive silting-up of the Loire and the fact that ships were tending to become larger combined to cause a decline in the activity of the port of Nantes, which held its own only with great difficulty. In 1856 the fore-port of Saint-Nazaire, which achieved independent status in 1879 was created; but Nantes still had to find a new way to the sea. With the digging of the lateral, maritime Loire canal from 1881 to 1892, traffic in the port of Nantes began to increase: the tonnage, which had fallen to 350,000 tons in 1890, rose to nearly two million tons in 1913; during the First World War, Nantes became the port of supply for the British and American armies and was the centre of considerable activity. The Second World War and the occupation left terrible scars on both city and port; fifteen hundred buildings were completely annihilated, three thousan partially destroyed and six thousand badly damaged one-third of the quays disappeared; thirty ships and floating dock were sunk in the Loire. Civilian casualtie (dead and wounded) were counted by thousands, bot at Nantes and Châteaubriant. All this destruction not withstanding, Nantes is today expanding rapidly. It still an art and tourist centre and has its university onc again; its industrial potential grows ever greater and th creation of the 'Autonomous Port of Nantes-Saint Nazaire' makes it the premier Atlantic port of Europe

Nantes has two monumental and noteworthy build ings, the château and the cathedral. The old residence o the dukes of Brittany was for a long time a militar building; nowadays, part of it serves as a museum o regional popular art and a museum of decorative art. I was ceded to the city in 1915 and soon cleared o additional buildings which had grown up inside, afte which it was restored and enhanced by a ring of lovel gardens and water-filled moats. In former days th curtain walls ran down directly to the Loire where postern gave access to the river. In shape an irregula square, the château still has almost all its fifteenth- an sixteenth-century towers. The explosion of a powde magazine in 1800 destroyed the Spanish Tower and th neighbouring buildings, including the chapel. Th west entrance, between the two big towers know respectively as the Bakery and the Hind's Foot, still ha its fifteenth-century drawbridge. Four other tower complete this group: the Jacobin Tower crowned wit battlements, the Horseshoe Tower, the River Towe and the Port Tower.

The courtyard inside, with its magnificent wellhead under a wrought-iron framework, is surrounded by buildings dating from different periods. The most interesting of these, the Grand Logis, constructed in the days of Duchess Anne, is crowned with magnificent, gabled dormer windows and richly gilded pinnacles; two storeys of Italianate loggias top the neighbouring elegant Pavilion of the Golden Crown with its double staircase. Another Renaissance building, known as the Small Government House, stands in the southeast corner of the courtyard, while on the west side, to the left of the entrance, stands the so-called Big Government House, which was rebuilt after the fire of 1670.

To the north of the château stands the Cathedral of Saint Peter, badly damaged during the last war. Its first stone was laid in 1434 and the church took four centuries to build, starting with plans by the Duke of Berry's architect Guillaume de Dammartin-sur-Yèvre and ending with the work of Sauvageot in 1893. During the fifteenth and the early sixteenth century the façade, the towers and the lateral chapels were built; the three naves were begun in 1518; then the work stopped and did not start again until the reign of Louis XIII. The unfinished building was turned into an arsenal and stables during the Revolution, and the construction was finished only between 1840 and 1893.

The façade has five doorways, two of them in the returns. In the middle is the Virgin's doorway, its tympanum carved with a Last Judgment; it is flanked by doorways dedicated to St Peter, St Paul, St Yves and the Youths of Nantes, the tympanum of the last named portraying the lifting of the siege of Nantes by Chillon.

There are charming carvings in the vaults of these doo ways, in particular singing angels. At the south corn of the façade is a pleasing exterior pulpit.

Inside, the tomb of François II and Marguerite d Foix, placed in the cathedral in 1817, is one of the maste pieces of early sixteenth-century sculpture. It is th work of Michel Colombe and his team of Tourai stone carvers and was designed by the painter Jea Perréal. The recumbent statues of the duke and th duchess lie on a table of black marble, their heads o cushions carried by three small angels. Two rows o sixteen niches decorate a block of white marble suppor ing the black table; in the upper row, of red marble, th niches are separated by arabesque-covered pilasters an enclose small statues of the Apostles and Saints (S Francis of Assisi, St Marguerite, Charlemagne and S Louis); the lower rows have female mourners, carve in green marble, with their heads, hands and feet i white marble. Finally, at the four corners of the tom large statues represent the cardinal virtues: the figure o Justice, thought by some to be a likeness of Duche Anne; Force, in armour and helmet; Temperanc holding a horse's bit; Prudence, two-faced as a youn woman and an old man. This work is so perfect an harmonious that it is difficult to decide what to admi most: fidelity of tradition discernible in the lovely fol of the cloth or the delicate Renaissance decoration.

There are many other sights in Nantes to satisfy th curiosity of visitors or to attract their attention. Fo instance, close to the château, a whole section of th medieval city with narrow streets and old houses su vives around the Church of the Holy Cross, built ov

The courtyard,
Château of Nantes

the ruins of a pagan temple. Almost everywhere there are late fifteenth- and sixteenth-century buildings of the brilliant ducal period, such as the Jean V Manor, the country house of the bishops where Duke Jean V died in 1399; the Psallette, a charming fifteenth-century edifice with a chamfered staircase tower; St Peter's Gate, a vestige of the old fortifications. The eighteenth century also has left Nantes with some large houses, thanks to the bounty of wealthy merchants and ship-owners: the old mansion of the Company of the Indies on La Fosse quay; houses built by architect Cerneray on the old Brancas and Flesselles quays; and on the former island of Feydeau some lovely groups of buildings such as the Villetreux mansion.

As Nantes' population has increased continually since 1850, new quarters have grown up around the city, which has been extended to take in neighbouring communes. Between the two world wars in the twentieth century, important town-planning works were carried out; two arms of the river were filled in, joining the Feydeau and Gloriette islands to the right bank, and the Loire flows now in two large arms, the Madeleine and the Pirmil. The course of the Erdre has been diverted; formerly, the river joined the Loire below the château, but now it runs in a long, underground canal situated upstream from the château, giving access to the Brittany canal. Big housing developments are being built almost everywhere around the city, on the islands and even on the left bank near the junction of the Loire and Nantes Sèvres. From 170,000 inhabitants in 1911, the population increased to 195,000 in 1936 and to 383,000 in 1969. The Nantes-Saint-Nazaire area now comprises 450,000 people and the figure is expected t reach more than one million by the year 2000.

Nantes has a great tradition in the field of highe education and cultural activities. Founded in 1460 wit a number of professors of canon law, law and medicin the university met with difficult times in the fifteent century, but it surmounted these, thanks to Charles VII With varying numbers of students, the university con tinued until 1735 when its two law schools were tran ferred to Rennes, to which the High Court of Brittan wished to attract institutions of that kind; the faculti of literature and medicine remained at Nantes. In 179 everything vanished. In 1962 the university was re established with four faculties, including that of leg and economic science where emphasis is placed on th teaching of maritime and aerial law. It should not b forgotten that Nantes was the birthplace of Jules Vern whose brilliant novels foreshadowed present-day ai and space exploration. The re-establishment of th university has increased the Nantes student body fro four to fifteen thousand.

From the economic point of view, Nantes already ha sugar refineries during the colonial era, to whic textile industries were added in the eighteenth centur and metallurgical plants in the nineteenth. The city industries experienced a big extension during the Fir World War, though they had fallen to the lowest poi at the time of the Liberation. Moreover, the promotio of Nantes to the rank of regional metropolis of the Loi country would seem to have given it considerabl increased importance and influence. Within the region administration the 'Regional Action Office' has bee

Staircase in a
venteenth-century house,
Avenue F.-Roosevelt,
Nantes

created responsible for gathering all the information and doing all the planning needed for the development of the region. In the same way, the 'Regional Chamber of Commerce and Industry' co-operates with the government services. Finally, in January 1970 the 'Western Economic Observatory' was set up at Nantes to serve three regions (the Loire country, Brittany and Poitou-Charente) by collecting and storing all possible statistical information and making all the necessary data available to meet the needs of the administration and private interests.

The industrial, economic and commercial development of the Loire estuary depends today on the 'Autonomous Port of Nantes-Saint-Nazaire' established on 1 April 1966. Within this new entity are grouped three formerly distinct maritime establishments: Nantes, Donges and Saint-Nazaire, three ports with different vocations, together with all other port installations in the estuary and the maritime reach of the Loire. As far back as 1903 and 1913 two legislative measures provided the basis for Nantes and its sea channel to become what they are today. In 1933, the digging of a canal to the petroleum port of Donges was declared a work of public utility; the shipyards of Saint-Nazaire, a port founded in the nineteenth century as a supplement to Nantes, began to build liners and cargo ships of the largest size, as well as giant tankers. Nantes, with its many kinds of industries, has at the very centre of its population a port with thousands of feet of quays and powerful dock installations. Quite large ships can reach Nantes by way of the channel, following the left bank up to Paimbœuf.

The maritime reach of the Loire extends from Nantes t Le Pellerin, its banks flanked by industrial establish ments at Chantenay, Basse-Indre, Indret and Couëro (foundries, metallurgical plants and tool factories) Since 1966, there has been a special quay at Chevire fo handling exotic woods. Downstream from Le Pelleri the surrounding country opens up; a low, dam alluvial plain stretches back from both banks of th river, especially towards the north where the outline o the distant foothills of Brittany can be seen. This i stock-breeding country.

Half-way between Le Pellerin and Donges, on th right bank, a big electric power station has been unde construction since 1966 on the island of La Calotte, an a vast amount of sand has had to be shipped in to ensur that it is above flood level.

On a rocky island near the left bank stands Paimbœuf it was once a centre of great activity, but nowadays it sole function is as port for cargoes connected with th chemical industry. Opposite Paimbœuf, the navigabl channel crosses the river in the direction of Donges.

Donges on its rocky island was no more than a sma village at the beginning of the twentieth century, wit one modest refinery; but its proximity to fairly dee water decided its destiny, although everything wa destroyed during the Second World War. The town ha now been rebuilt a little to the north; the roof of it curious church rests on parabolic arches, and the granit walls of the buildings are lighted by wide stained-glas windows; outside, the façade is embellished wit cement sculptures retracing the episodes of the life o Christ. The port of Donges provides a quay capable o

Thatched cottage on the Grande Brière Island

Donges petrol refinery,
from Paimbœuf

The Loire
at Saint-Nazaire

accommodating at one time five ships with up to 75,000 tons total load. In 1969 the port handled nine million tons of goods, this figure consisting of imports of raw materials and manufactured goods, as well as exports of the latter. Downstream from Donges, a channel six miles long gives access to sizeable ships whatever the state of the tide; it follows the north bank as far as Saint-Nazaire.

The port of Saint-Nazaire is magnificently situated facing the sea at the mouth of the Loire; it cannot, however, be reached by just any line of approach, for the sands of the Loire have created a vast underwater delta, with submerged rocks, so that ships have to utilize the Charpentier passage along the north shore; it is constantly being dredged to ensure passage to fair-sized ships. Until 1865 Saint-Nazaire was nothing more than a fishing port; after construction of the first dock communicating with the sea, the port developed steadily until the Second World War, during which it was totally destroyed; it was rebuilt somewhat further to the west, in a more suitable position, and is now both a commercial port and a big shipbuilding yard. The commercial port is very well equipped with storehouses, refrigeration depots and ship-repairing facilities, and is a base for seagoing tugs.

Saint-Nazaire's shipyards, capable of building and repairing the largest ships, are meeting Japanese competition by modernizing their equipment and methods. Many of the shipyard workers live outside the town to the north, in La Brière; this is an immense marshy region formed by partial filling-in of a sea gulf existing in Tertiary times, with a scattering of many small islands formed from volcanic rocks (Fedrun Island, Joachim Island, etc.) on which people now live. All the houses which were formerly thatched, now have slate roofs.

In 1968, traffic using the autonomous Nantes-Saint-Nazaire port complex reached the figure of 11,554,000 tons, thus placing it fifth among French ports. In its capacity as a transit port, it distributes throughout the Loire region, and even to the Parisian region, its imports of early vegetables, citrus fruit, exotic woods, etc., while its exports consist of manufactured products, cereals, sugar and metals, particularly tin.

As an industrial port, it serves the big industrial complex centred in the Nantes-Saint-Nazaire metropolitan area. In ten years, movement of goods in this area has doubled, but this satisfactory achievement has not prevented the autonomous port from making ambitious plans for the future, which include big improvements in the channel leading to the ports of Nantes (ships up to 20,000 tons) and Donges (ships up to 120,000 tons); new kinds of repair facilities for ships at Saint-Nazaire; new industrial zones to be created in the port areas; and reorganization of the Saint-Nazaire shipbuilding yards to prepare them for the construction of giant 500,000-ton tankers.

Harbour entrance and quay,
Saint-Nazaire

Conclusion

At the end of this journey of more than six hundred miles, looking over the pictures taken by Hélène Jeanbrau of places hitherto unknown, or recorded by her camera from an unusual angle, one is astonished that it is still possible to make so many discoveries along the Loire. The journey also proves the extent to which the river and its valley have for centuries served as a road for the diffusion of civilization, religion and culture, from the Mediterranean to the Atlantic, thus acting as a unifying and reconciling force between regions so distinct from each other in soil, people and natural resources. One is also struck by the qualities of application and tenacity shown by the diverse peoples in the different parts of the valley – a region famous for the insouciance of its inhabitants – who have constructed so many outstanding monumental buildings, châteaux, churches and abbeys, or rebuilt them from their ruins. These same good qualities, together with inventiveness and a spirit of enterprise, applied in the economic sphere – agriculture, industry, commerce – have made the valley, at least at certain periods, one of the richest and most prosperous regions of France.

The new sources of energy being developed along the banks of the Loire, the policy of decentralization which has now been in force for some years, ambitious plans for urban development which have been carried through, and the establishment of new universities and other cultural centres, all these make it possible today to predict for the Loire, its valley and its hinterland a future worthy of their glorious past.

Index